SHAPES
IN MATH, SCIENCE AND NATURE

Squares, Triangles and Circles

Written by CATHERINE SHELDRICK ROSS

Illustrated by BILL SLAVIN

KIDS CAN PRESS

Acknowledgments

Thanks are due to the many people who made these excursions into the nature of some key mathematical shapes possible. To start with, academic and public libraries have been indispensible in making available to me hundreds of essential books and articles, especially these: Thomas F. Banchoff, *Beyond the Third Dimension* (1990); Keith Critchlow, *Order in Space* (1969); H. Martyn Cundy and A. P. Rollett, *Mathematical Models* (1961); Alan Holden, *Shapes, Space and Symmetry* (1971); Hugh Kenner, *Bucky: A Guided Tour of Buckminster Fuller* (1973); Spiro Kostoff, *The City Shaped* (1991); Peter Pearce, *Structure in Nature is a Strategy for Design* (1978); Marjorie Senechal and George Fleck, eds. *Shaping Space: A Polyhedral Approach* (1988); and Peter S. Stevens, *Patterns in Nature* (1974). Thanks also to the many children who helped test out the activities and to Jacob Ross, who read various versions of the manuscripts and made great suggestions. And a special thanks to the team at Kids Can Press who were co-creators of this whole series — Valerie Wyatt and Laurie Wark, who provided the inspired editing; Michael Solomon, who did the book design for *Circles*; Esperança Melo, who combined type and illustration into integrated spreads; and Bill Slavin, whose genius at illustration has brought the text to life.

Text © 2014 Catherine Sheldrick Ross
Illustrations © 2014 Bill Slavin

Compiled from the following books:
Circles © 1992
Triangles © 1994
Squares © 1996

Kids Can Press acknowledges the financial support of the Government of Ontario, through the Ontario Media Development Corporation's Ontario Book Initiative; the Ontario Arts Council; the Canada Council for the Arts; and the Government of Canada, through the CBF, for our publishing activity.

Published in Canada by
Kids Can Press Ltd.
25 Dockside Drive
Toronto, ON M5A 0B5

Published in the U.S. by
Kids Can Press Ltd.
2250 Military Road
Tonawanda, NY 14150

www.kidscanpress.com

Original editions edited by Laurie Wark
Original editions designed by Michael Solomon and Esperança Melo
This edition based on the design by Studio Link

This book is smyth sewn casebound.
Manufactured in Buji, Shenzhen, China, in 11/2013, by WKT Company

CM 14 0 9 8 7 6 5 4 3 2 1

Library and Archives Canada Cataloguing in Publication

Ross, Catherine Sheldrick
[Works. Selections]
    Shapes in math, science and nature : squares, triangles and circles / written by Catherine Sheldrick Ross ; illustrated by Bill Slavin.

Includes index.
Contents: Circles — Triangles — Squares.
Ages 9–14.
ISBN 978-1-77138-124-6 (bound)

    1. Shapes — Juvenile literature. 2. Circle — Juvenile literature. 3. Triangle — Juvenile literature. 4. Square — Juvenile literature. 5. Geometry — Juvenile literature. 6. Geometry in nature — Juvenile literature. I. Slavin, Bill, illustrator II. Ross, Catherine Sheldrick. Squares. III. Ross, Catherine Sheldrick. Triangles. IV. Ross, Catherine Sheldrick. Circles. V. Title.

QA445.5.R66 2013   j516'.15   C2013-906704-3

Kids Can Press is a **corus**™ Entertainment company

SHAPES

IN MATH, SCIENCE AND NATURE

CONTENTS

SQUARES   8

1. AMAZING SQUARES   10

The square up close   10

Making squares   12

Area of a square   14

Squaring off   16

Square numbers   18

A square story   19

Square illusions   20

Jacob's ladder   21

Square puzzlers   22

2. LIVING IN SQUARES   26

Grids   27

Grid art   27

Square cities   28

City squares   30

Square buildings   32

Square mazes   34

3. SQUARE DESIGNS   36

Tumbling blocks   37

Printing with squares   38

Jeu de parquet   40

Origami   42

Tangram   45

Polyominoes   46

4. CUBES   48

Cornered   49

Make a cube   50

Dicey counting   51

The Delian cube legend   52

Cubic puzzlers   53

Cuboctahedron construction kit   54

Prisms and antiprisms   56

Cubic architecture   60

Cubic bubbles   62

TRIANGLES 64

I. AMAZING TRIANGLES 66

Making triangles 67

Keeping in shape with triangles 68

The triangle up close 69

Angles 70

Adding up the angles 71

Cutting the angles in half 72

Area of a triangle 73

Triangular numbers 74

Pascal's triangle 75

Phantom triangles 76

2. SPECIAL TRIANGLES 78

Right triangles 78

Ancient geometry 79

Measuring height 80

Isosceles triangles 81

Paper airplane math 82

Surveying by triangulation 83

Triangle trees 84

Equilateral triangles 85

Equilateral designs 86

Fold an equilateral triangle 87

Triangle weave 88

Dissection puzzle 90

Triangle fractals 91

Hexaflexagon 92

3. BUILDING WITH TRIANGLES 94

Putting triangles to work 95

Bridges 96

Railway bridges 97

Monuments 99

Buildings 100

Roofs 101

4. TRIANGULAR PRISM 102

Make your own kaleidoscope 103

Make a construction kit 104

Platonic solids 106

Newton's prism 108

Grow an alum crystal 109

S. TETRAHEDRON 110

Make a tetrahedral gift box 111

Tetrahedral puzzlers 112

Bucky building 114

Toothpick architecture 115

Alexander Graham Bell and the tetrahedron 116

6. PYRAMIDS 118

Leonardo's parachute 119

Make a pyramid 120

The Egyptian pyramids 121

Aztec pyramids 121

CIRCLES 122

1. AMAZING CIRCLES — 124

Giotto's O — 124

Drawing circles — 125

The circle up close — 126

Fold some circles — 127

Measuring circles — 128

Easy as pi — 129

Make a Moebius strip — 131

2. LIVING IN CIRCLES — 132

Circle prints — 134

Building in circles — 136

The super circle — 137

3. FAR-OUT CIRCLES — 138

Make an ellipse — 140

The expanding circle trick — 141

Stone circles — 142

Make a sundial — 144

4. SPHERES — 148

The big blue ball — 149

Mapping Earth — 150

Bubbles — 151

Bubble packing — 152

Let's play ball! — 154

Losing your marbles — 155

Super domes — 156

5. DISKS — 158

Chip disks — 159

Pinwheel disks — 160

Super flyer — 161

Tops — 162

Wheels — 164

6. CYLINDERS — 166

Be an architect — 167

Castles — 168

Tricks with cylinders I — 169

Tricks with cylinders II — 170

7. CONES — 172

Cone hats — 173

Slicing a cone — 174

Hyperbola folding — 175

8. SPIRALS — 176

Party spiral — 177

Fibonacci numbers — 177

Oh, sunflower! — 178

A-mazed — 179

Answers — 180

Formulas — 183

Glossary — 184

Index — 186

SQUARES

If you stand with your arms stretched out, you're about as tall and as wide as a square. A square is a shape with four equal sides and four equal angles. Look around and you'll see lots of square shapes — checkerboards, waffles, floor tiles and square window panes. The rooms of your home are probably either squares or rectangles. You may live on a street that's part of a square city block. Even in rock paintings and in the earliest writing systems, the square was used as a symbol for the house or settlement.

People used to believe that the square was lucky and had magical powers. In the Middle Ages, Europeans would wear a silver disk with a square cut into it on a necklace to protect them from the Black Death plague.

Squares are flat. But if you put six squares together in the right way, you get a cube. You can find cubes in nature as crystals, such as the salt crystals you put on your vegetables. Architects like cubes for building because cubes can fit together side by side or they can stack, like blocks, into high-rise towers.

If you find a square word you don't understand, check the glossary on pages 184–185 for an explanation.

1. AMAZING SQUARES

The number four is the most important thing about the square. Every square has four sides of equal length. And every square has four equal angles. Do the square test on this book — it looks sort of square, with four sides and four equal angles. To know for sure if it's a square, you'll have to measure to see if the four sides are exactly the same length.

THE SQUARE UP CLOSE

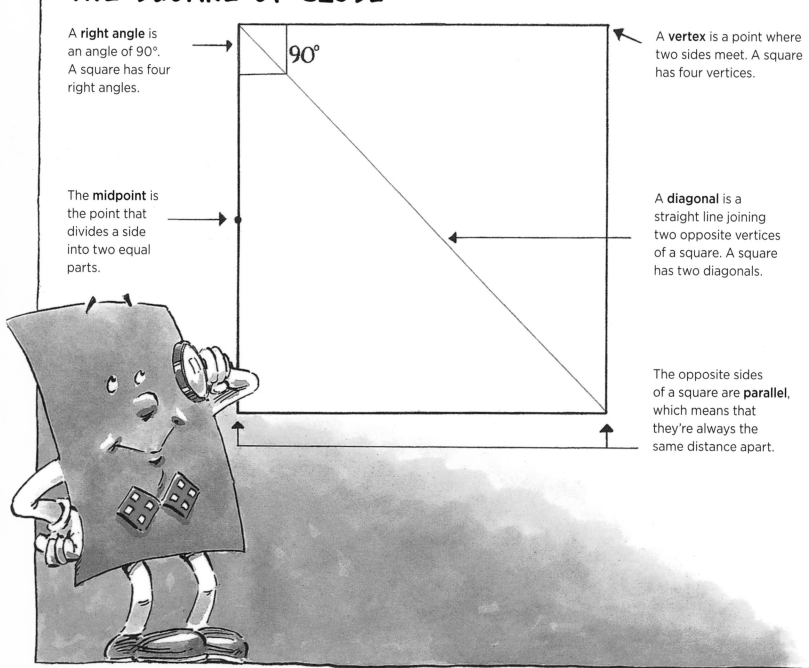

A **right angle** is an angle of 90°. A square has four right angles.

90°

A **vertex** is a point where two sides meet. A square has four vertices.

The **midpoint** is the point that divides a side into two equal parts.

A **diagonal** is a straight line joining two opposite vertices of a square. A square has two diagonals.

The opposite sides of a square are **parallel**, which means that they're always the same distance apart.

What is a square?

Mathematicians use lots of fancy terms to describe a square. A square is a **quadrilateral**, which means it's a polygon, or closed shape, with four sides. A square is also a **rectangle** — a quadrilateral with 4 right angles. A square is a **parallelogram** — a quadrilateral with opposite sides that are parallel. And, finally, a square is a **rhombus**, which is a parallelogram with four sides the same length.

CLOSED SHAPE WITH FOUR SIDES? ✓

FOUR RIGHT ANGLES? ✓

OPPOSITE SIDES PARALLEL? ✓

FOUR SIDES THE SAME LENGTH? ✓

You can figure out how far it is around the outside of a square (its perimeter) by multiplying the length of one side by 4.

MAKING SQUARES

Since the days of the cave-dwellers, people have been making squares — drawing them on cave walls, carving them into stone and using them to decorate temple walls. You can draw a square freehand. But if you want a perfect square, here are two methods that work every time.

Folding a square

You'll need:

- a rectangular piece of paper, such as printer paper or a sheet of newspaper
- scissors

I. Fold a short side of the paper so that it exactly touches a long side to make a triangle.

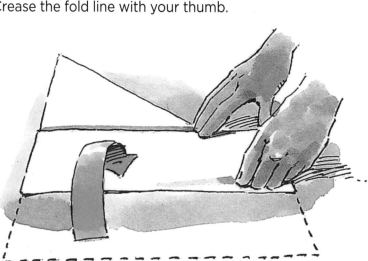

2. Fold the remaining paper over the triangle. Crease the fold line with your thumb.

3. Unfold the paper and cut off the extra piece along the creased fold line.

4. You now have a square. The fold line dividing the square into two equal triangles is a diagonal of the square.

Drawing a square

You'll need:
- a piece of paper
- a ruler
- a pencil
- a compass

1. Use a pencil and ruler to draw a straight line at least 5 cm (2 in.) from the bottom edge of the paper. Mark each end of this line with a dot and label this line AB. This line will be the lower side of your square.

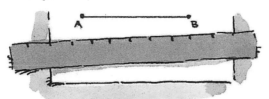

2. Extend the line AB to a point called C so that BC is about 4 cm (1½ in.) long.

3. Set the compass opening to the same distance as BC. Put the compass foot on point B. Draw an arc to intersect AB at D.

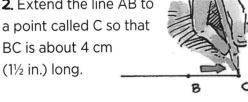

4. Make the compass opening a bit larger and put the compass foot on point D. Draw two arcs above and below the line.

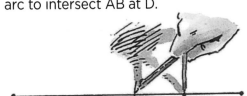

5. Without changing the compass opening, put the compass foot on point C. Draw a second pair of arcs above and below the line to cut, or intersect, the first arcs.

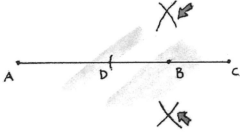

6. Use your ruler to draw a line through the two points where the arcs intersect, or meet. Extend the line toward the top of the paper. You have just made a 90° angle here — the first corner of your square.

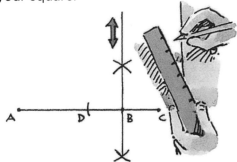

7. Set the compass opening to AB (remember that's the length of the side). Put the compass foot on point B and draw an arc above the base line to cut the vertical, or up-and-down, line at E.

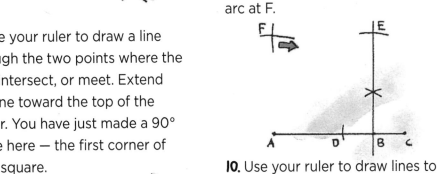

8. Without changing the compass opening, set the compass foot on E and draw an arc.

9. In the same way, set the compass foot on A and draw a second arc, intersecting the first arc at F.

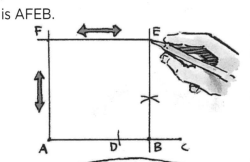

10. Use your ruler to draw lines to join AF and FE. Your square is AFEB.

> You can skip steps 2 to 6 if you have a set square to make the right angle. Just line up the set square as shown.

AREA OF A SQUARE

If you ever have to carpet the floor of a square tree house, here's how you can tell how much carpet to buy. You have to be able to figure out the area of the square, but luckily that's easy. All you do is multiply the length of one side of the square by itself. So if the square floor has a side that's 3 m (10 ft.) long, then the area of the square is 3 times 3, or 9 square meters (100 square feet).

Now that you've mastered the basics of working out the area of a square, here are some fancy tricks you can do with areas.

Doubling the square

Draw a diagonal line through a square. Use this diagonal as the side for a second square. This second square is always twice as big as the original square. This means that the area of the square drawn on the diagonal is two times the area of the original square.

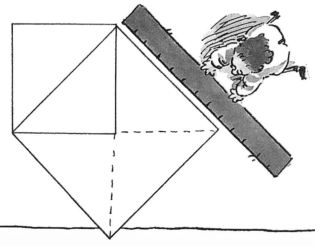

Square multiplication

Here's a way to multiply the size of a square to double, triple or quadruple it, or even make it ten times as big as the original square.

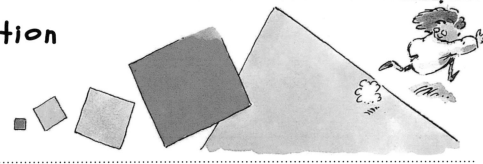

You'll need:

- paper
- a pencil
- a ruler
- a compass

1. Start with a small square ABCD drawn in the bottom corner of a piece of paper.

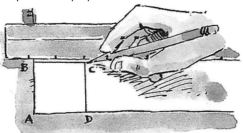

2. Draw the diagonal of the square AC and extend the line.

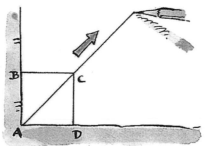

3. Extend the line BC right across the paper to form the line BE.

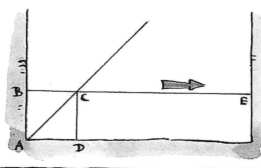

4. Put the compass foot on A and the pencil on C. Draw an arc to touch the bottom of the paper at F. The line AF is the side of a second square that's twice as big as your original square. Draw this square.

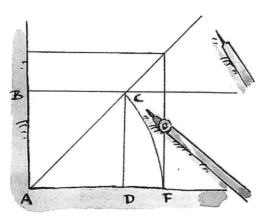

5. To triple the original square, put the compass foot on A and the pencil on the point where BE cuts the right side of the second square. Draw an arc. The point where the arc touches the bottom of the paper is the bottom right-hand corner of the third square.

6. There are two secrets to drawing all the next squares. First, always keep the compass foot on A. Second, put the pencil on the point where BE cuts the right side of the previous square and draw an arc to touch the bottom of the paper. Eventually you'll go right off the paper.

Squaring off

Can you turn five small, equal-sized squares into one large, perfect square? The big square will, of course, have to be five times the size of the small square. Check it out for yourself.

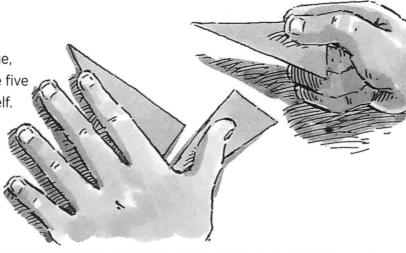

You'll need:
- a piece of paper
- a ruler
- a compass
- a pencil
- scissors

1. Draw five identical squares in a row with sides of 3 cm (1 in.).

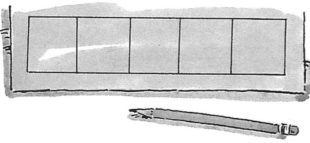

2. Cut out the row of five squares.

3. Cut off two squares. Draw a diagonal line through the two squares as shown and cut along the diagonal line.

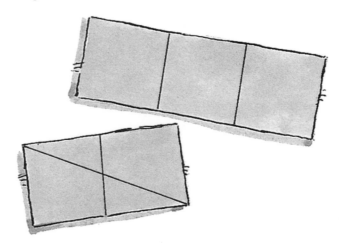

4. Repeat step 3 with a second set of squares.

5. Use the five pieces to make a single, perfect square. (See page 180 for the answer.)

FOUR SQUARE

Squares are associated with lots of things that come in fours. Very old maps show Earth as a flat square, with the four winds coming from the four compass points of north, south, east and west. In some mythologies, four pillars on a square base hold up the whole world. Ancient legends often describe Earth as a square, with a giant or angel at each corner. In a Yucatan Indian myth, four ancestors at each corner of the square world hold up the heavens.

SQUARE TALK

Real square

Back to square one

A square meal

A square deal

Winning fair and square

A square peg in a round hole

Squaring accounts

SQUARE NUMBERS

You can use a handful of pebbles or coins to unlock the secrets of square numbers — the same way Pythagoras did 2500 years ago. Pythagoras was a Greek mathematician who studied numbers by arranging pebbles into different geometric shapes. Arrange your pebbles into square shapes like these.

With his pebbles arranged into square numbers, Pythagoras subtracted each square number from the next one in the series. This means he subtracted 1 from 4 to get 3; 4 from 9 to get 5; 9 from 16 to get 7 and so on. He discovered an odd pattern — can you find it? (See page 180 for the answer.)

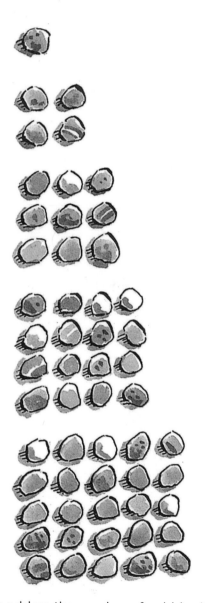

If you add up the number of pebbles in each square arrangement, you get the first five square numbers: 1, 4, 9, 16, 25. What are the next five square numbers? It's easy to figure out once you spot the pattern. To get the square number, you square the number, or multiply it by itself: 1 × 1 = 1; 2 × 2 = 4; 3 × 3 = 9; 4 × 4 = 16 and so on to 9 × 9 = 81 and 10 × 10 = 100. So the first ten square numbers are: 1, 4, 9, 16, 25, 36, 49, 64, 81, 100.

A SQUARE STORY

According to an old story, the Shah of Persia was very impressed with a new game called chess that had just been invented. So he summoned the inventor to give him a reward. "Name it and it's yours," said the Shah. All the inventor asked for was some wheat. "Give me one grain of wheat on the first square of the chess board, twice as much on the second square, twice as much again on the third square and so on, doubling each time, to the 64th square." "Only some wheat? But you can ask for anything — how about some silver plates or golden goblets? Wouldn't you like a herd of fine camels?" But the inventor said he was a simple man and wanted only wheat.

Imagine the Shah's surprise and annoyance when he discovered that it would take more wheat than he had in his whole kingdom to keep his promise. The number of grains of wheat mounts up fast when you keep doubling. On the eighth square, there are 128 grains of wheat; on the ninth square, there are 256 grains; on the tenth square, there are 512 grains; and on the thirty-first square, there are over a billion grains of wheat.

SQUARE ILLUSIONS

Hermann grid

The Hermann grid is a tricky optical illusion of black square blocks separated by white lines, or streets. Hold this illustration at arm's length and look at the black blocks. At the intersections of the white streets, can you see a faint gray dot? The gray dot is an optical illusion caused by the contrast of black and white. The white looks whiter when it's surrounded by black. The white in the streets has more contrasting black around it than the white in the intersections. Check this out. Cover up the black blocks so that you can see only one street. What happens to the gray dots?

Target practice

Is this a square or not? Check the sides against a ruler to find out.

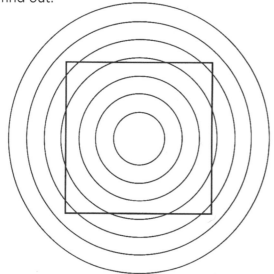

Which is bigger?

1. If this were a square cake, which piece would you rather have if you were very hungry — the square piece inside or the amount that's left over when you take the square piece away?

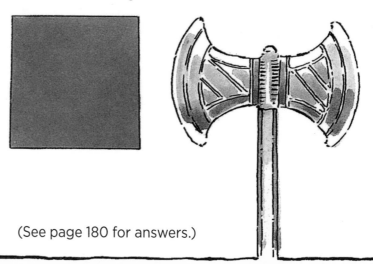

2. Which diagonal is longer — the diagonal of the square or the diagonal of this Cretan double ax?

(See page 180 for answers.)

Jacob's ladder

Decorate your Christmas tree the way the early pioneers did, with homemade ornaments. This accordion shape, called a Jacob's ladder, is an easy decoration to make. Fold two paper strips into interlocking squares, put a thread through it and hang it up.

You'll need:
- 2 contrasting colors of construction paper
- scissors
- white glue

1. From one piece of construction paper, cut four or five strips about 3 cm (1 in.) wide. Glue together enough strips to make one piece about 1 m (3 ft.) long.

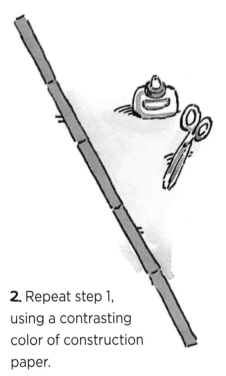

2. Repeat step 1, using a contrasting color of construction paper.

3. Put some glue on one end of one of the strips. Place this gluey end on top of one end of the other strip, so that the strips form a right angle.

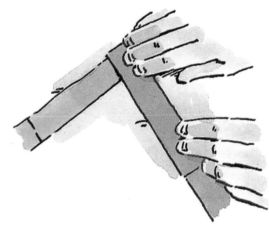

4. Fold the bottom strip over the top strip.

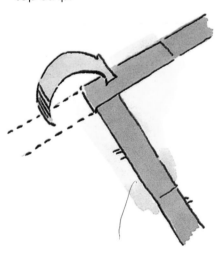

5. Repeat step 4, folding the bottom strip over the top strip, until you run out of paper. You should end up with interlocking squares, folded on top of each other like an accordion.

6. Trim off any extra paper, and glue the last two squares together.

SQUARE PUZZLERS

You'll need to put your thinking cap on before starting this foursome of square puzzles. (See page 180 for the answers.)

How many squares?

To make this brainteaser, start with a square piece of paper.

1. Fold the square of paper in half and sharpen the fold line between your thumb and first finger. Open the paper.

2. Repeat step 1, folding the square of paper in half in the other direction.

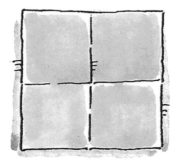

3. Fold each side to touch the midline and sharpen the fold line. Open the paper each time before folding the next side. You now have a square of paper folded into 16 small squares.

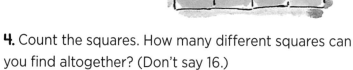

4. Count the squares. How many different squares can you find altogether? (Don't say 16.)

What's my shape?

This puzzle is a shape-changer — from square, to cross, to loops, to what?

You'll need:

- a square piece of paper (any size will do, but a very small square of paper is best)
- scissors
- sticky tape

1. Fold the square piece of paper in half.

2. Fold it in half again in the other direction to make a smaller square.

3. Cut out a small square on the sides away from the fold lines.

4. Unfold the paper, which will now be in the shape of a cross.

5. Tape the ends of the cross together to form two loops at right angles to each other.

6. Cut along the original fold lines. Can you guess what shape you'll get? Get out your scissors to find out.

Square dissection

Can you turn a square into a triangle?

You'll need:
- a piece of thick paper or cardboard
- a compass
- a ruler
- a pencil
- scissors

1. Following the instructions on page 13, make a square with sides 10 cm (4 in.) long.

2. Mark the midpoint of each side.

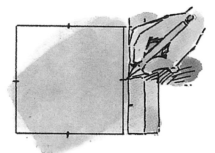

3. Connect the midpoints of two adjacent, or touching, sides.

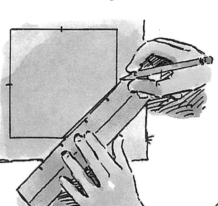

4. Mark the place where a diagonal cuts the line you made in step 3 and call this point P.

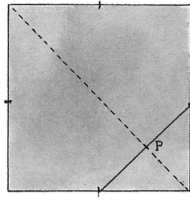

5. Draw lines from P to the midpoints of the opposite sides.

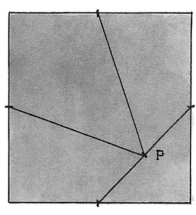

6. Cut along the three lines so that you end up with four pieces.

7. Reassemble these four pieces to make a triangle.

Why are squares so hard to find?

Because they're never a-round.

Square takeaway

These 24 toothpicks are arranged into a large square with nine smaller squares inside. Can you remove six toothpicks so that there are only two squares left inside?

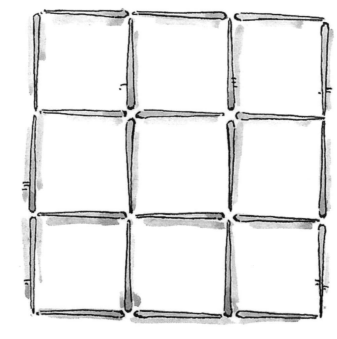

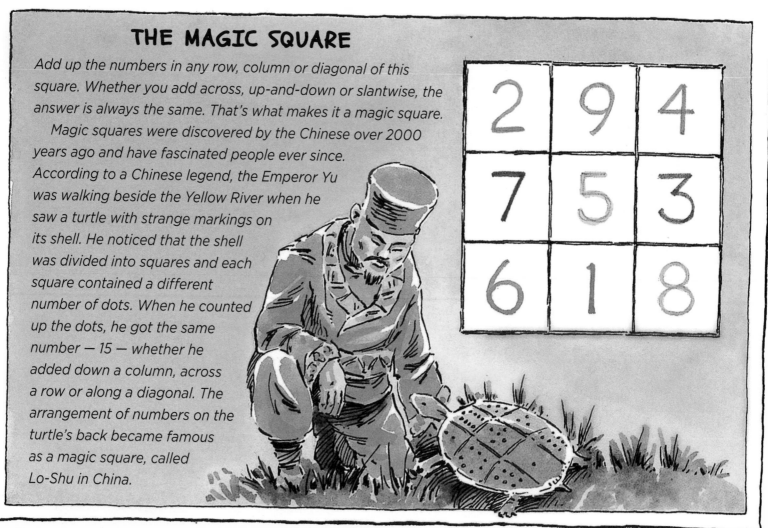

THE MAGIC SQUARE

Add up the numbers in any row, column or diagonal of this square. Whether you add across, up-and-down or slantwise, the answer is always the same. That's what makes it a magic square.

Magic squares were discovered by the Chinese over 2000 years ago and have fascinated people ever since. According to a Chinese legend, the Emperor Yu was walking beside the Yellow River when he saw a turtle with strange markings on its shell. He noticed that the shell was divided into squares and each square contained a different number of dots. When he counted up the dots, he got the same number — 15 — whether he added down a column, across a row or along a diagonal. The arrangement of numbers on the turtle's back became famous as a magic square, called Lo-Shu in China.

2	9	4
7	5	3
6	1	8

2. LIVING IN SQUARES

Imagine that you're a city planner about to design a new city. You'll need to draw a city plan, including streets and buildings. Don't forget to add some open spaces for parks. Chances are you'll draw square blocks and add some square buildings. Your city plan might look a bit like this one, painted on a wall in Turkey around 8500 years ago. The square houses are laid out in straight lines.

Unlike birds who hollow out nests into round shapes and beavers who build domed houses, human beings usually live in spaces that are shaped into squares. Read on to find out why the square has given its shape to many famous buildings and cities since ancient times.

Grids

Guess which cities are easier to find your way around — cities laid out in square blocks or cities where a tangle of streets grew up from old cow paths? The city built on the square grid design, of course. Why? First, because grids are so simple — at every intersection, two straight lines cross each other without bending. And second, the squares formed by the intersecting lines are all identical. So every block is the same size and it's the same distance from one intersection to the next. Look at a map for the place where you live, and you'll probably see lots of squares.

Grid art

Do you have a picture that you want to make bigger? No problem, if you use a square grid. On your original picture, draw a grid of squares as shown. Then decide how much bigger you want the copy to be. To make it twice as high and twice as wide, draw a grid of squares with a side twice the length of the original square. Then copy the picture, square by square.

You can stretch the picture lengthwise, if you make a grid from rectangles 2 units high and 1 unit wide.

And you can distort the picture in weird ways, if you do this.

You can stre-e-e-tch the picture sideways, if you make a grid from rectangles 1 unit high and 2 units wide.

SQUARE CITIES

This 4500-year-old ceramic pattern from India shows two ancient town plans. Both are based on the square and the number four. Since then, the square has been nearly everybody's favorite shape for town planning.

4500-year-old town plans from India

Rome was called a squared city. When the Romans extended their empire into Europe and beyond, they brought their square plans with them. They reshaped the existing settlements into squares and they built new square settlements according to standard plans. The most basic plan was the *castrum* or military camp. It was designed on a grid plan with a small square at the center where troops assembled.

Roman military camp

Here's one layout for a square city that fortunately was never built. In 1619, a philosopher, Johann Andreae, developed this maze-like plan for an ideal city, called Christianopolis. If you were in the outside square, how would you get to the center?

Johann Andreae's plan for an ideal city

Circleville, Ohio, started off in 1810 as a circular city. But the square won out, little by little. By 1856, nothing remained of the circle that gave the town its name.

1837

1838

Circleville, Ohio, 1810

1849

1856

SURVEYING

The lines we see in nature are all curves. Look at the outlines of coastlines, riverbeds, ponds, forests and mountain ranges and you won't see a single right angle or straight line. But when the Spanish, French and English settlers came to the forests of North and South America, they brought the right angle with them. They mapped out, or surveyed, the landscape into squares. This map shows one of the first townships surveyed in Ohio, United States, around 1785. Surveyors were told to lay out square townships and one-square-mile farms. But as you can see, the surveyors couldn't make the river follow a straight line.

29

CITY SQUARES

Is there a town or city square where you live? Squares are great places for people to gather. Some city squares have developed all by themselves at the crossing of two important roads. And sometimes city planners design a square for the town center right from the beginning.

Lots of squares are just as famous as the cities they're in — there's St. Peter's Square in Rome, St. Mark's Square in Venice and Red Square in Moscow. Some squares aren't even square, actually being longer than they are wide! Here are some remarkable city squares.

Aztec capital at Tenochtitlan

In 1519, when Hernan Cortés and his Spanish soldiers reached the Aztec capital (now Mexico City), they found a city twice the size of the largest city in Spain. At the center of this city was a ceremonial plaza made of polished stone. This plan, probably drawn by Cortés, shows a central square on an island surrounded by water and connected to the mainland by causeways. Within three years, Cortés completely destroyed the city.

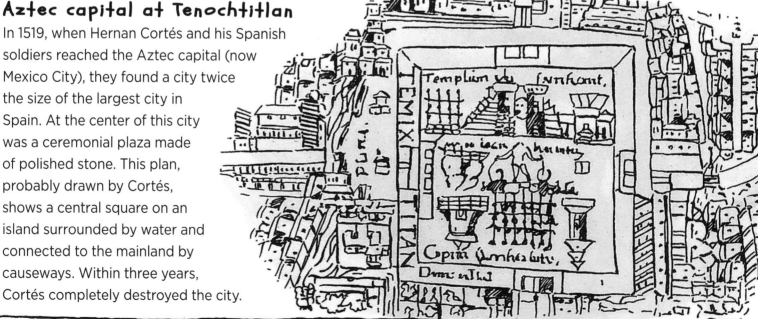

Grenade-sur-Garonne in France

Mathematicians must have planned this market square. The market block at the center of this French town is a perfect square. But each block to the east or west of the center block gets progressively bigger. The secret to the distance between the blocks is that the length of each block is the diagonal of the smaller one beside it.

Tiananmen Square in Beijing

China had no tradition of public squares. But in 1949 the Communist leader Mao Zedong built a square in Beijing about the size of 90 football fields — so huge that a crowd of a million loyal farmers and workers could meet to wave flags and cheer his speeches. In 1989, Chinese students held a giant protest against the government in Tiananmen Square.

Red Square in Moscow

Russia's most famous gathering place is Red Square in Moscow, where the May Day parades are held each year. From Red Square, you can see the Great Kremlin Palace, which was built for the ruling Czars and now houses the President of Russia.

SQUARE BUILDINGS

Although most people were sold on square and rectangular buildings, the 19th-century American builder Orson Squires Fowler thought that the perfect form was the circle. Since circular houses are so hard to build, Fowler decided the next best thing was the octagonal building. Fowler built his own octagonal mansion at Fishkill, New York, and soon the fad for building Fowler octagons spread across North America. In the 19th century, people built octagonal houses, schools, churches and even barns. For most of human history, however, people have found the square a more practical shape for buildings. Check out some of these amazing square buildings from around the world.

Le Corbusier's museum of unlimited extendability

Seen from above, this museum looks like a maze. Le Corbusier's concept for a museum called for inner walls made from the same-sized units that could be put together in different ways. This meant that the walls could be moved around and changed to make inside spaces that would suit the exhibits. The National Museum of Western Art in Tokyo, Japan, is a real-life example of Le Corbusier's concept for a museum.

Santa Sophia

The Emperor Justinian completed the great church, Santa Sophia, in Constantinople (now Istanbul) in the year 537AD. It has a square central space inside that's covered by the great circular dome above.

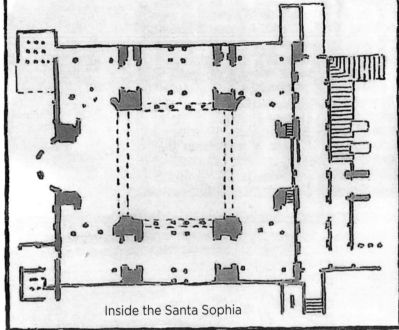

Inside the Santa Sophia

Santa Sophia, now called Hagia Sophia, was converted into a mosque in 1453, and then a museum in 1935.

Japanese houses

For more than a thousand years, the Japanese have used tatami to cover the floors of their houses. What's a tatami? It's a thick piece of matting that is the shape of two squares, set side by side. A single tatami is the right size to sleep on, about 2 m (6 ft.) long and 1 m (3 ft.) wide. When the Japanese design their houses, they use the tatami as a measuring unit. There are 4-tatami rooms, 4½-tatami rooms, 8-tatami rooms, 10-tatami rooms and so on.

A 4½-tatami room

SQUARE MAZES

Mazes are tricky spaces that are easy to get lost in. Can you find the path to the center of these square mazes? Turn to page 180 for the solutions.

Church maze

This pavement maze in the abbey of St. Bertin at Saint-Omer in France was destroyed in the 18th century because it was too much fun. The noise of people running through the maze distracted attention from the church services.

Garden maze

This design for a garden maze by G. A. Boeckler was published in 1664. It is a true puzzle maze: unlike the St. Bertin maze, it has branching paths and dead ends.

THE GOLDEN RECTANGLE

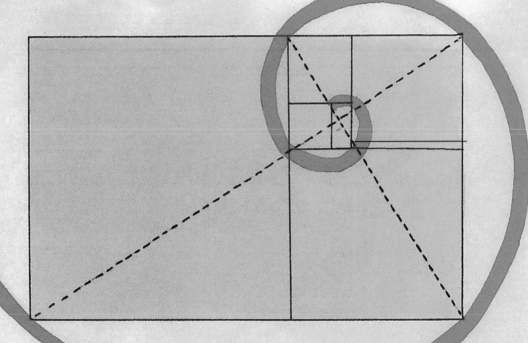

Some people think the golden rectangle is the most pleasing shape possible because they like its proportion of length to width. The ancient Greeks thought so and used the golden rectangle shape for building the Parthenon in Athens. Modern artists also like the shape and so most picture frames are golden rectangles.

To get a golden rectangle, you start with a square and find the midpoint of the base. Then you put the compass foot on this midpoint and the pencil on an opposite vertex. Draw an arc to intersect the line that extends from the base of the square. This intersection point is one corner of the golden rectangle.

It's easy to turn a golden rectangle into a spiral — you make more golden rectangles. To the first rectangle, attach a square with a side equal to the long side of the rectangle. Now you have a second, bigger golden rectangle. Continue attaching squares to the long side of the golden rectangles and you get a shape made of squares that spiral outward in ever-widening turns. This is the shape of regular growth in nature — when living things grow, their bodies become bigger but the parts keep the same proportions. So a snail shell gets bigger as it grows, but it always has the same shape.

3. SQUARE DESIGNS

The square is about the simplest shape you can make, with its repetition of equal sides and right angles. But if you're making a design that uses squares, don't worry that all the good ideas have been used up. Thousands of different square designs are possible.

Take a look at some square designs from all over the world, from cave drawings to the most modern art. These designs have decorated walls, fabrics, quilts and canvases.

The cross was an ancient sign of great power long before it became a Christian symbol. This is a Jerusalem cross.

In this ancient Egyptian design, the square takes 90° or quarter turns.

The Maya built great temples based on geometric forms. Squares decorate the walls of the Maya temple of Uxmal in Yucatan, Mexico.

The walls of the Alhambra, the Muslim palace in Granada, Spain, are covered with intricate, geometric patterns like this one.

The Dutch artist Piet Mondrian just couldn't stop painting squares. He gave his pictures names like "Place de la Concorde" and "Composition with red," but to most people the paintings look like squares and rectangles.

Quilt makers in North America a hundred years ago created this illusion of tumbling cubic blocks by using a single diamond piece arranged into a hexagon. The secret is to use three shades of color in the same position throughout the quilt — one light, one medium and one dark.

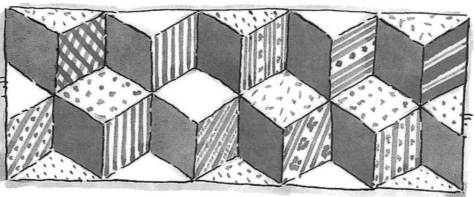

Tumbling blocks

Make your own tumbling blocks pattern.

You'll need:

- 3 colors of Bristol board
- a pencil
- a compass
- a ruler
- scissors

1. Use the compass to draw a circle — 5 cm (2 in.) is a convenient compass opening to use. Without changing the compass opening, mark off six division points on the circle.

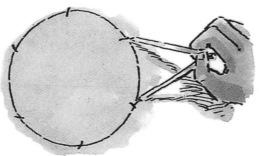

2. Use your ruler to draw lines to connect the division points. You have made a hexagon.

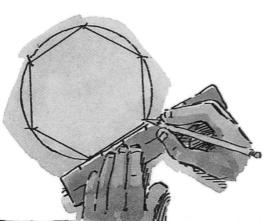

3. From the circle's center, draw a line to every second division point to make three diamonds.

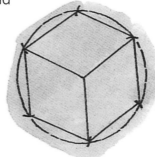

4. Cut out the diamonds.

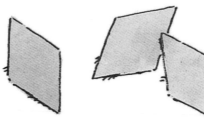

5. Repeat steps 1 to 4 to make more diamonds. You'll need at least four diamond shapes in each color of Bristol board to make this tumbling blocks pattern.

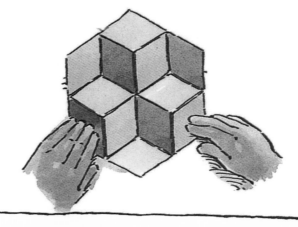

Printing with squares

Here's a quick way to use your favorite square pattern for making wrapping paper.

You'll need:

- white paper
- corrugated cardboard (the kind used for grocery cartons)
- a pencil
- a ruler
- a set square
- scissors
- white glue
- 2 or 3 paintbrushes
- 2 or 3 contrasting colors of tempera or poster paint
- newsprint or other paper to print your design on

1. Draw a square on white paper — sides of 8 cm (3 in.) work well. Cut out the square.

2. Fold the square in half once and in half again to make a small square. Unfold.

3. Fold the square in half once along the diagonal and in half again to make a small triangle. Unfold.

4. Cut along the fold lines so that you get eight right-angled triangles. To design a printing pattern in which half the area of the original square is colored, throw away four triangles and use the other four triangles to make a pattern.

5. Try arranging the triangles in different ways to decide on a pattern for your print. (There are 13 different patterns possible. After you've experimented to discover the pattern you like best, check page 180 to see if you've thought of all of them.)

6. On corrugated cardboard, draw two squares the same size as the original paper square. Cut them out.

7. On one cardboard square, trace the design you decided on in step 5. Cut out the pieces.

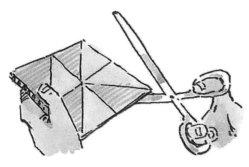

8. Paste the pieces onto the second cardboard square to make a stamp for your design. When you print the pattern, the raised parts will be colored and the rest will stay white.

9. Use different brushes to apply two or three colors of paint to the raised parts only.

10. Press the stamp onto the paper you are making into wrapping paper.

11. Reapply paint. Stamp the paper again alongside the first impression. Continue, until you cover the whole paper with the design.

If you hold the stamp the same way up each time, you get a design like the one in step 11 — called a *translation* or a *slide*. For variety, turn, or rotate, the stamp to get a design like this.

SAND DESIGNS

These designs in sand aren't made by artists but by vibrations of high-pitched sound. To make these designs, called Chladni figures, a physicist puts a little sand on a glass or metal plate. Then she places two fingers on the plate and, at the same time, draws a bow, like a violin bow, along the edge of the plate. The bow makes the plate vibrate, and the vibration causes the sand to shake itself into a pattern. As you can see, square plates produce square-looking sand designs with 90° angles.

Jeu de parquet

People in France used to play the game of parquet on a small table, using 64 porcelain square tiles of two colors. With this set of 16 squares, you'll still be able to make millions of different patterns with no repetitions.

You'll need:

- a square box, such as a chocolate box
- black Bristol board
- plain white paper
- stiff cardboard, such as the backing of a notepad
- a ruler
- a pencil
- scissors
- a pin
- glue

I. Take the top off the square box and set the top aside. Measure the length of the side of the bottom part of the box.

2. Subtract 0.5 cm (¼ in.) from this length. Draw a square on a piece of black Bristol board, using this shorter measurement as the length of the side. Cut out the square.

3. Cut out a square from white paper to be the same size as the black square.

4. Fold the white square into 16 small squares (see "How many squares?" on page 22). Sharpen each crease between your thumb and forefinger.

5. Place the white square over the black square so that it matches exactly.

6. Use a pin to poke a hole on the fold line, close to one edge of the square. Make sure that the pin goes through the two layers. Repeat this step so that you make a pinhole in three places along each side, on the fold lines.

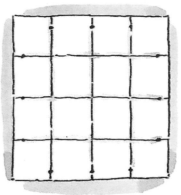

10. Paste one white triangle on each black square to make a design unit.

7. Set aside the white square until step 9. Use a ruler and pencil to draw lines on the black square to connect the pinholes. You should now have a grid of 16 squares.

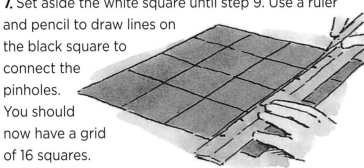

11. Put the 16 design units into the square box. Start with the pieces all aligned the same way.

8. Paste the large black square onto a stiff piece of cardboard. Cut out the 16 black squares.

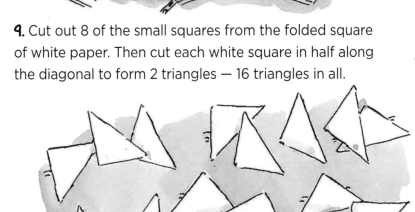

12. Now make your pattern. There are four possible positions for each square piece. Experiment by rotating the pieces until you produce a knock-out design.

9. Cut out 8 of the small squares from the folded square of white paper. Then cut each white square in half along the diagonal to form 2 triangles — 16 triangles in all.

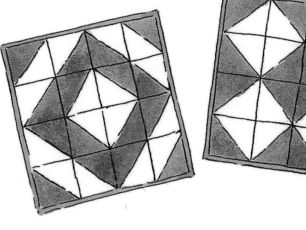

ORIGAMI

Take a square and turn it into a bird, a fish, a box or a boat. You don't need to be a magician. You just need to know the craft of origami, which is the ancient Japanese art of paper folding. Read the rules below, then make the origami crafts on the next pages.

Basic rules of origami

I. Work on a hard, flat, clean surface.

2. You'll need a square of paper — a square of 15 cm (6 in.) works well. If you don't have origami paper, many other kinds will work such as notepaper, gift paper or pages from a magazine, as long as the paper is cut into a square. The paper needs to be strong enough to be folded repeatedly without tearing or stretching. If you're using origami paper, place the colored side face-down at the beginning.

3. Make every fold as straight as you can. Then run your thumbnail over the fold to make a sharp crease.

Fortune teller

1. Fold a square of paper in half diagonally. Unfold. Fold the paper in half diagonally the other way. Unfold.

2. Fold all four corners in to touch the center, where the diagonal folds cross each other.

3. Turn the paper over. Fold all corners to touch the center.

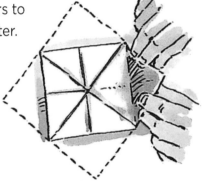

4. Fold the square in half so that the square flaps face out.

5. Fit your thumbs and forefingers into the compartments under the square flaps on each side and pinch. You can open and close this shape in two directions.

6. To add pizzazz, color the inside eight triangles in two contrasting shades such as red and green.

7. Turn your origami shape into a fortune teller by writing eight messages under the flaps — one message on each triangle. Next write the numbers from 1 to 8 on the top of the flaps.

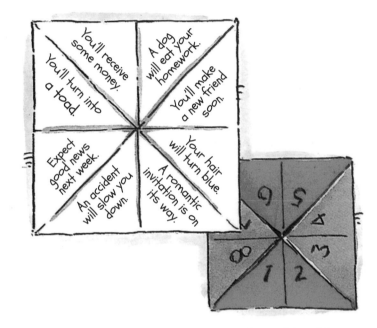

8. Now you're ready to tell a fortune. Get a friend to pick a number from 1 to 8. Open and close the fortune teller that many times. Now ask your friend to pick one of the exposed numbers on the flap. Read out the fortune under the chosen flap.

Whale

1. Fold a square of paper in half diagonally from corner to corner. Unfold.

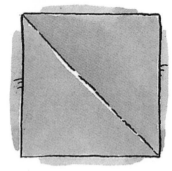

2. Fold one of the other corners in to touch the diagonal.

3. Repeat step 2 with the last corner.

4. Turn the shape over so that the flaps are underneath. Fold it in half along the diagonal line you made in step 1.

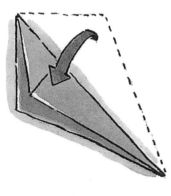

5. Fold the nose back along the diagonal fold line as shown. Crease and unfold. Push the nose inside the body by folding along the line you just made.

6. Fold the tail up. Crease and unfold.

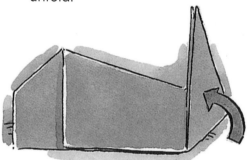

7. Pick up the head of the whale in one hand, with your forefinger and thumb along the center crease. With your other hand, push the center crease along the tail inside the body. Fold along the crease line you made in step 6 to tuck the tail up and inside the body.

8. To make the flippers, fold the flaps back.

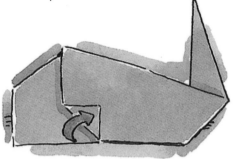

9. Cut part of the way down the center crease of the tail. Fold down to make fins.

10. You can hang your whale from a lightweight stick to make a mobile.

44

Tangram

This tangram puzzle comes from China, where it is called Chi-Chiao, meaning "The Seven Clever Pieces." After you've cut these seven clever pieces from a square, you can use them to make a face, camel, whale, house, cat, sailboat — in fact, hundreds of different shapes.

You'll need:

- stiff cardboard or Bristol board
- a pencil
- a ruler
- scissors

I. On the cardboard, draw a square. For the side of the square, choose a length that is a multiple of four — for example, 16 or 20 cm (8 in.).

2. Using your ruler, make marks that divide the sides of the square into four equal segments. Draw faint lines to divide the large square into 16 small squares.

3. Draw lines as shown.

4. Cut out the seven pieces and you're ready to make these shapes or to invent your own.

Stumped on some of these shapes? Turn to page 180 for some answers.

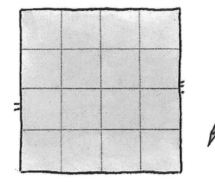

POLYOMINOES

You likely know about dominoes, which are made from two identical squares connected along an edge. But how about trominoes (three squares), tetrominoes (four squares) or pentominoes, formed from five identical squares? An American puzzle mathematics professor, Solomon Golomb, invented the word "polyomino" to mean any set of identical squares connected along an edge.

Cut out four identical squares and use them to experiment with polyominoes. There is only one arrangement of squares to make a domino. There are only two ways to join three squares together to make a tromino — three squares in a row and an L shape. But there are five different tetrominoes — can you find them? (See page 180 for the answer.)

If a shape can be turned over to fit over another shape, the two shapes are considered mathematically the same.

Pentominoes

With the 12 different pentominoes that can be made from 5 squares, you can make a game for two players.

You'll need:
- paper
- cardboard or Bristol board
- a pencil
- a ruler
- scissors
- glue

To make the game pieces

1. Cut a square out of paper — 20 cm (8 in.) makes a convenient size.

2. Carefully fold the square of paper exactly in half and sharpen the fold line between your thumb and first finger. Open the paper. Fold the square of paper in half in the other direction and sharpen the fold line. Open the paper.

3. Fold each side to touch the midline and sharpen the fold line each time. Open the paper each time before folding the next side. You now have an unfolded square of paper divided into 16 small squares.

4. Fold the paper in half twice to make a smaller square. As in step 3, fold each side to touch the midline and sharpen the fold line each time. Unfold the paper.

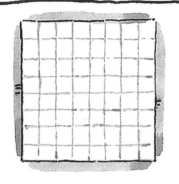

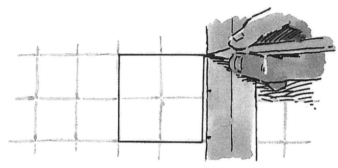

5. Use your pencil and ruler to outline the four squares in the middle.

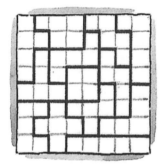

6. Follow the pattern shown here to outline all 12 pentominoes. Check that each shape you outline really is made from 5 squares.

7. Paste the square of paper on a piece of cardboard or Bristol board. Cut out the square from the cardboard.

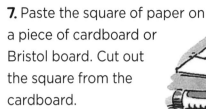

8. Trace the outline of this square onto another piece of cardboard. Cut out the second cardboard square and set it aside to use as your game board.

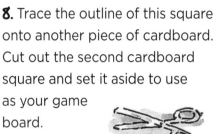

9. Cut up the first cardboard square into the 12 pentominoes. Throw away the square piece from the middle, which you outlined in step 5.

To play the game

1. Each player in turn picks a pentomino piece and places it on the board.

2. The object of the game is to prevent the other player from putting another piece on the board.

3. The player who makes the last move wins.

If you don't have a player to play against, use the pentomino pieces to solve these tricky puzzles. The bar is 3 squares wide and 20 squares long. The rectangle is 6 squares wide and 10 squares long. Each foot of the bridge is 3 squares wide. (See page 181 for answers.)

4. CUBES

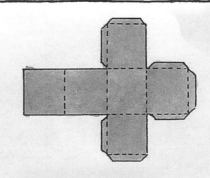

If you roll a cube on a table, no matter how it lands it always looks the same. Unless you paint the faces different colors or mark them like dice, you can't tell which way is up or down and which way is front or back. Each cube has six same-sized square faces and, of course, they all meet at 90° angles.

This outline might look like a hopscotch pattern, but mathematicians call it a net and you can use it as a pattern to make a cube.

Check out cubic crystals for yourself. Examine a crystal of salt under a strong magnifying glass.

Architects like cubes because they fit together so well. Cubes pack together to fill space completely without leaving any air holes in between. If oranges were cube-shaped instead of spherical, they would fill all the space in the orange crate and not just three-quarters of it.

Cubes happen in nature, too. A fossil sponge is hollow but its supporting structure looks like the edges of a cube. Salt crystals are cubes and so is metallic iron. Both salt and iron are built up of very tiny building blocks that are cube-shaped. These building units are too small to see, but at the Brussels International Exhibit in 1958, the basic unit of iron was magnified 200 000 times to make a gigantic sculpture. To make the shape more dramatic, the sculptor tipped the cube onto one vertex.

Cornered

Turn a flat piece of paper into a three-dimensional shape to find out the secrets of a cube's corners, or vertices.

You'll need:

- paper
- scissors
- sticky tape

I. Fold a square piece of paper into quarters.

2. Cut a line from the midpoint of one side to the middle of the square.

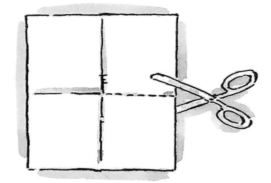

3. Now you are ready to experiment with shapes. Arrange three squares around a single point by overlapping the two squares that you cut apart in step 2. You get a closed corner, or vertex.

4. Arrange four squares around a single point and you have no corners, just a flat piece of paper.

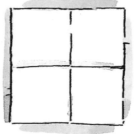

5. How about five squares? If you cut out a fifth square the same size as the others, you can tape it into the cut opening. Now all five squares fit around a single point, but again you don't have a corner. You have a saddle shape that folds in and out.

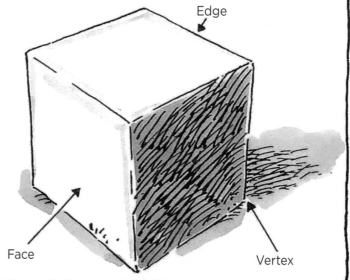

What's happening?

As you can see, squares can fit together in only one way to enclose space and make a corner — you need three squares to fit around a single vertex. Six squares fit together to make a cube with six faces, eight corners or vertices and twelve edges.

Edge

Face

Vertex

Make a cube

Once you get the hang of making cubes, you can make them in different sizes from tiny to quite big. You can jazz up your cube with colored markers for a gift box or write numbers on it to make a die. You can even print a pattern on your cube (see "Printing with squares" on page 38). Just remember that it's easier to decorate *before* you glue the faces together.

You'll need:

- an index card
- Bristol board or thick paper
- a compass
- a pencil
- a ruler
- scissors
- white glue
- colored markers (optional)

1. In one corner of an index card, draw a square with 6-cm (2½-in.) sides. Cut out the square. You'll use this cardboard shape as a pattern to draw six squares on Bristol board or thick paper.

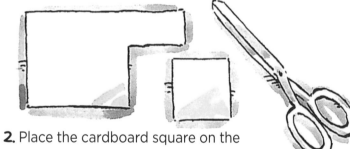

2. Place the cardboard square on the Bristol board and mark the four corners of the first square. Use a ruler to draw the lines.

3. Draw the other five squares the same way, in the pattern shown, to make a net.

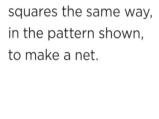

4. Draw seven tabs as shown, about 0.5 cm (¼ in.) wide.

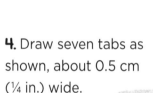

5. Lightly score the fold lines with the compass foot. This will make it easier to fold. But don't push too hard.

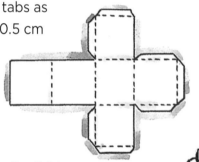

6. Cut out the net.

7. Crease the fold lines with your thumb. If you want to decorate the faces of your cube, now is the time to do it.

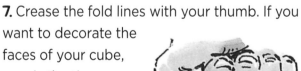

8. Put glue on the two tabs on one side-square, and attach to make a corner.

9. When this corner is dry, put glue on the two tabs on the other side-square and attach to make another corner.

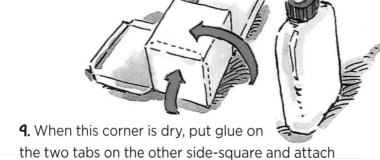

10. When this corner is dry, put glue on the final three tabs and attach the last face of the cube.

> Make a bunch of boxes in graduated sizes and in different colors, and you have a nested set of gift boxes that fit inside each other. But don't glue the top flap down if you want to get the inside boxes out again.

Dicey counting

This magic trick will amaze your friends, even math whizzes. It's based on the fact that each opposite pair of faces on a die adds up to 7.

You'll need:
• three dice

1. Ask a friend to stack three dice in a column.

2. Turn your back while your friend adds up the numbers on the five hidden faces.

3. When your friend is ready, turn around, glance at the top face of the column of dice and quickly say, "Abracadabra, the answer is 17."

How does it work?

The answer in this case is 17. Each opposite pair of faces on a die adds up to 7. So you know that the sum of the top and bottom faces on three dice is 3 × 7 or 21. You can see at a glance that the top face is 4. Therefore, the hidden faces must be 21 minus 4, which is 17. If the top face were 6, the answer would be 21 minus 6 or 15.

THE DELIAN CUBE LEGEND

In 430 BC, a plague of typhoid fever swept over the Greek city of Athens. According to legend, the Athenians consulted the oracle at Delos for advice. The answer came back, "Apollo is angry. You must double the size of his altar here at Delos before the plague will end." The altar was in the shape of a cube. So the Athenians made a second cube identical to the first and set it alongside. The new altar was double in volume but, alas, it was no longer cube-shaped. This made Apollo angrier and he sent an even worse plague.

So the Athenians made a new cube, with edges twice as long as the edges of the original altar. Apollo got even angrier. What went wrong the second time? To find the volume of a cube, you multiply the length of the edge by itself three times. So if the original altar had a side that was 2 units long, its volume would be 2 times 2 times 2, which is 8 cubic units. When the Athenians doubled the length of the altar's side to 4 units, the volume of the new cube became 4 times 4 times 4, which is 64 cubic units — eight times as big. So instead of doubling the size, the Athenians had built a monster-altar, eight times the size of the original. Yikes! Check this out for yourself, using sugar cubes. If you use two sugar cubes for the length of a side, how many sugar cubes does it take altogether to make a cube?

The bad news for the Athenians is that the problem set by Apollo can't be solved. It's one of the mathematical impossibilities of the ancient world. It is impossible to double the cube if your only instruments are a compass and straight edge.

CUBIC PUZZLERS

If you don't find square puzzles challenging enough, here are some puzzles that add a whole extra dimension. (See page 181 for the answers to these cubic puzzlers.)

Cube cuts

Suppose you have a 3-cm (1-in.) wooden cube. What is the smallest number of saw cuts you would have to make to get 27 cubes with 1-cm (½-in.) edges?

Cross-sections of the cube

How would you slice a cube to get these shapes?

a square

a triangle

a hexagon

Coloring a cube

Suppose you wanted to color the faces of a cube so that each face is one solid color and no adjacent, or touching, faces are the same color. What is the smallest number of colors needed?

Rotating a cube

If you take a flat coin and spin it around, you get the outline of a sphere. What shape do you get if you hold a cube on vertices along the long diagonal and spin it around?

a rectangle

Ask your parents if they remember the Rubik's Cube. In 1975, a Hungarian architect, Ernö Rubik, invented this tricky cube made of 27 smaller cubes. Hungarian teachers used the Rubik's Cube as a teaching aid in schools before it became a puzzle craze that swept the world.

Cuboctahedron construction kit

With this construction kit, you can make cubes, cuboctahedra, square-based pyramids and other shapes.

You'll need:

- Bristol board or cardboard in at least two colors
- a pencil
- a ruler
- a compass
- scissors
- a one-hole punch
- a box of 5-cm (2-in.) elastics

1. On a piece of Bristol board or cardboard, draw a square with 10-cm (4-in.) sides. Use the compass foot to score the lines outlining the square.

2. Draw a slightly larger square as a 0.5-cm (¼-in.) frame around the first one. Cut out the larger square.

3. Punch a hole at each corner of the small square. Trim the corners and fold up the edges along the score lines.

4. Make more square units the same way, using the same color of Bristol board. You'll need 6 square units to make a cube.

5. Now make a triangular unit, using a different color of Bristol board. Start by drawing a straight line 10 cm (4 in.) long. Put the compass foot on one end of the line and draw an arc as shown, keeping a compass opening of 10 cm (4 in.). Without changing the compass opening, put the compass foot on the other end of the line and draw a second arc to intersect the first one. Draw two lines to make the other two sides of the triangle.

6. Use the compass foot to score the lines outlining the triangle.

7. Draw a slightly larger triangle as a 0.5-cm (¼-in.) frame around the first one. Cut out the larger triangle.

8. Punch a hole at each vertex of the small triangle. Trim the corners and fold up the edges along the score lines.

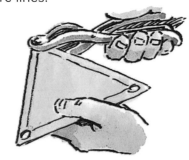

9. Make more triangular units the same way, using the same color of Bristol board.

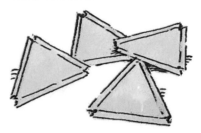

Cube

1. Start by lining up two squares as shown. Join them by fitting an elastic over the punched holes.

2. Use three more elastics and two more squares to make a four-sided column.

3. With four elastics, attach a square unit to form a top. Use another four elastics to attach the last square to complete the cube.

Cuboctahedron

Jazz things up with a special shape called a cuboctahedron — it's like a cube with the corners sliced off. Use six squares of one color and eight triangles of a contrasting color.

1. Use an elastic to attach a triangle and a square together. Make a second triangle-square unit the same way.

2. Arrange these two triangle-square units around a single vertex so that the squares and triangles alternate. You've just made one vertex, or corner, of the cuboctahedron. In total, the cuboctahedron has twelve identical vertices, each one surrounded by two squares alternating with two triangles.

3. Use elastics to add more faces. Just make sure that you alternate squares and triangles so that the side of a triangle is always connected to the side of a square.

....

Square-based pyramid
Use 1 square and 4 triangles.

Here are some more neat shapes you can make with your construction kit.

Triangular prism
Use 3 squares and 2 triangles.

Rhombicuboctahedron
Use 8 triangles, 6 squares of one color and 12 squares of a second color.

Prisms and antiprisms

When you think of prisms, you may think of a triangular piece of glass that breaks up the sunlight into rainbow colors. But the word "prism" really refers to a shape. A cube is a prism. A prism must have a base and a top that are parallel and the same size and shape, and the sides of a prism must be parallelograms. To identify a prism, count the sides in the prism's base — three sides make a triangular prism, four sides make a rectangular prism, five sides make a pentagonal prism and so on. The cube is a rectangular prism, in which all the faces are same-sized squares. Experiment with this cube made out of straws. Afterward you can turn it into another neat shape called an antiprism.

You'll need:

- a package of plastic straws
- paper clips
- pins

I. Start by making the connectors for the vertices of the cube. For each connector, join three paper clips. Make eight connectors.

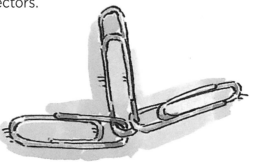

2. Fit two straws over the outside clips of one connector.

3. Fit an outside connector clip into the open end of these two straws.

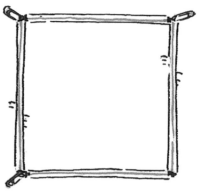

4. Make a square by fitting two more straws over the other outside clip on each connector.

5. Use a fourth connector to attach the last corner of the square.

6. Fit a straw over each of the four middle clips.

7. Now finish the job by adding the other four connectors and four more straws.

8. Your cube is ready to stand up. Oops! What happened? Very likely your twelve connected straws fell flat on the table in an interesting pattern. Move it a bit and you get another interesting pattern, but not a cube.

9. What to do? Add a triangle, which is the only structure that can't be pushed out of shape. Use a straw and two pins, as shown, to make the triangle. Make sure that the triangle you make contains a 90° angle.

10. Keep adding straws to make triangles, as in step 9, until the cube is rigid and won't wobble out of shape. What is the least number of straws you need to make the cube stand up? Check page 181 to see if you're right.

To make an antiprism

Now that you've made a square-based prism, you can turn it into a square antiprism. You discovered that the top and bottom faces must be lined up perfectly in a prism, one exactly above the other. In an antiprism, one of these faces is given a turn. Each vertex of the top face ends up directly above the midpoints of the sides of the bottom face.

1. Start with the straw cube you made on page 56. Keep the two triangles that brace the top and bottom faces but remove the four triangles that brace the sides.

2. Add an extra paper clip to the eight connectors making the vertices of the cube.

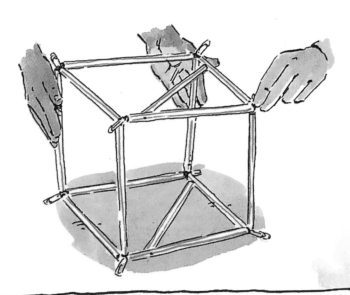

3. Fit four straws over the extra paper clips on the top face.

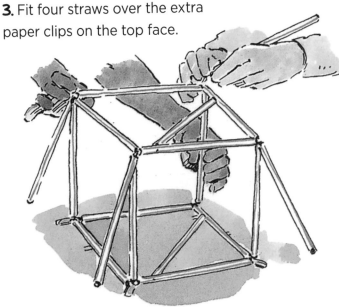

4. Attach the other ends of these four straws to the extra paper clips on the bottom face. There you have it — a square antiprism. As you see, this square antiprism has only two square faces. All the other faces are equilateral triangles.

Hmmm. 2 square faces, 8 triangular faces ...

IMPOSSIBLE CUBES

In 1934, a Swedish high school student, Oscar Reutersvärd, was doodling in the margins of his Latin text. He started with a six-pointed star, added some cubes and — presto! — an impossible object. You can draw it on paper, but you can never make it with real blocks. You could try by stacking up the column of blocks on the right, but then how could you arrange the other two rows of blocks?

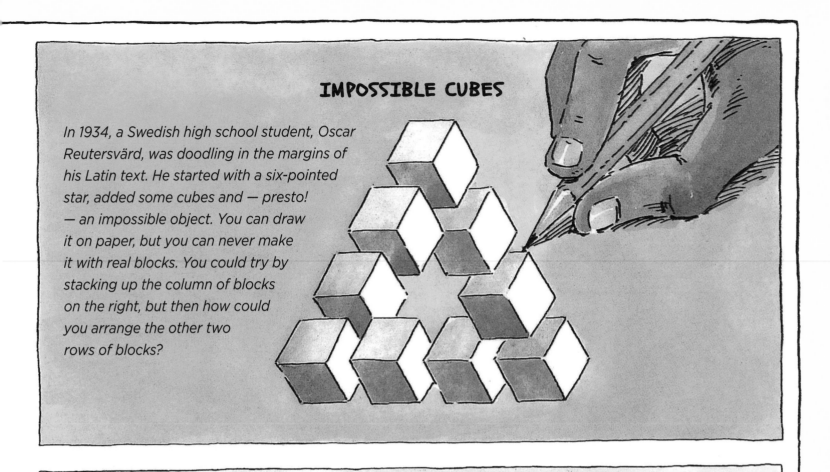

F + V = E + 2

What is this — a secret code? A recipe for ice cream? Actually, it's Euler's formula, discovered by Leonhard Euler (pronounced "oiler"). This formula shows us the relationship between the number of faces, vertices and edges that works for every kind of polyhedron — yep, every single one. The number of faces (F) plus the number of vertices (V) equals the number of edges (E) plus 2. Check this out on the cube — 6 faces + 8 vertices = 12 edges + 2.

CUBIC ARCHITECTURE

Anyone who has ever played with blocks knows that cubes fit together perfectly to fill space. Most other solid shapes fit together leaving big gaps and air holes in between. Cylindrical cans of soup waste space on the grocery store shelf because of the spaces between the cans. But cartons in the shape of cubes or rectangular prisms pack together efficiently to use up all the room on the shelf. Architects like to pack cubes together too. And when they get bored stacking cubes into straight columns, they try some variations. Here are two unusual buildings made from cubes.

Safdie's Habitat

Moshe Safdie designed this housing project for Expo '67, the World's Fair in Montreal, Canada. Each of these apartments is a cubic module that was built in a factory and then assembled on site. Putting the cubes together was like fitting together Lego blocks.

Sharon Temple

The Sharon Temple, north of Toronto, Canada, was modeled after King Solomon's temple from the Old Testament. It is built from three cubes set on top of each other like three tiers of a wedding cake. The square walls represent the four Gospels and the four directions of north, south, east and west.

Cubic bubbles

All bubbles are perfect spheres, right? Not when you start with a cubic bubble frame. Here's how.

You'll need:

- wire that's thin enough to bend and thick enough to hold its shape
- wire cutters
- a piece of corrugated cardboard (the kind used for grocery cartons)
- scissors
- a ruler
- a pencil
- a compass
- a glass jar
- bubble mixture

I. Draw a square with sides of 4 cm (1½ in.) on the piece of cardboard and cut it out. You'll use this square as a pattern to make the faces of the wire cube.

2. Cut a length of wire about 90 cm (35 in.) long. Start by forming a 10-cm (4-in.) double loop to be a handle. Twist the wire end around a few times to secure it.

3. Let the wire extend straight about 3 cm (1 in.) past the join of the handle. Give the wire a 90° turn to the right.

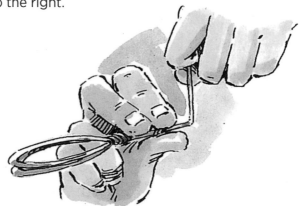

4. Use the cardboard square as a guide to bend the wire to make the bottom face of the cube. When you reach the vertex that completes the square, twist the wire around.

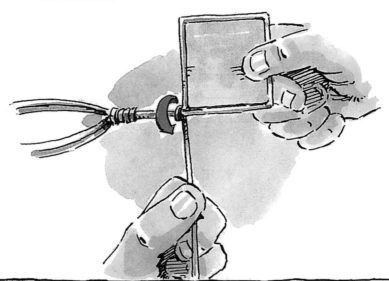

5. Next, make a vertical face in the same way, using the cardboard square to measure the length of the sides. You'll find that, for some edges, you end up with two strands of wire. Twist the two strands around each other so that the edge is as neat as possible.

6. Complete the six faces of the cube. Cut off any extra wire and secure the end by twisting it around.

7. Pinch the corners to make the frame as close to a cube shape as you can. (If it isn't perfect, it will still work.)

8. Put some bubble mixture into a glass jar.

> You can make a bubble mixture by gently adding 30 mL (2 tbsp.) of dishwashing detergent to 250 mL (1 c.) of lukewarm water. Try not to make a lot of suds.

9. Dip the cubical frame into the jar of bubble mixture, pull it out and prepare for a surprise. You probably have a square in the middle. When you put the frame back in the bubble mix, try to trap an air bubble inside the bubble frame. This time you should have a small cube right at the center of the bubble frame. Experiment to see the sizes of cubic bubbles you can make with your cubical frame.

What's happening?

Soap films always contract to form what mathematicians call a "minimal surface." Normally when you blow bubbles, the minimal surface is a sphere. But when the soap film forms on a cubical frame, the minimal surface turns out to be this terrific shape with a square or cube in the center.

What happens if ...

• you blow gently on the cubic bubble at the center of the bubble frame?
• you blow harder and the bubble floats free of the frame? What shape do you get?

TRIANGLES

Have you ever noticed how many interesting things come in threes? There are the three little pigs, the three Musketeers, the three Wise Men, three wishes and "three strikes — you're out." In fairy tales, it's third time lucky. Think of tricycles, triceratops, Napoleon's tricorn hat, the trillium, the three-leaf clover and, of course, the triangle with three sides and three angles.

Triangles are flat — they have only two dimensions. But if you put four triangular sides, or faces, together into a closed shape, you get a tetrahedron. Take a flat triangle and stretch it up to give it some thickness, and you have a triangular prism shape, like the prism that Newton used to split light into the colors of the rainbow. Arrange four triangular sides onto a square base, and you get a pyramid shape, like the great Egyptian pyramids.

When you read the Triangles section, you'll find out how triangles are used to measure heights and distances, make some mind-bending puzzles to wow your friends, discover why builders can't get along without triangles, learn about Alexander Graham Bell's tetrahedral kites, make a kaleidoscope, grow a crystal with eight triangular faces, and much more.

If you find a triangle word you don't understand, check the glossary on pages 184–185 for an explanation.

1. AMAZING TRIANGLES

Three dots are all you need to make a triangle. Just make sure the dots you draw are not in a straight line and then connect the dots. As you can see, triangles have three sides and three angles. Triangles are simple, elegant and strong and turn up when you least expect them. The triangle spider weaves her web into a triangular shape. The desert tortoise grows its shell in a hexagonal pattern made from six triangles.

That's why they're called tri-angles — *tri* is the Greek word for "three."

Making triangles

Find out about different kinds of triangles by making some from strips of cardboard and paper fasteners. When you're finished, save the cardboard strips for finding out about angles (see page 70) and for testing out your engineering savvy (see page 96).

You'll need:
- Bristol board in three different colors
- a ruler
- a pencil
- scissors
- a one-hole punch
- a package of paper fasteners

1. From one color of Bristol board, cut at least ten strips that are 8 cm (3 in.) long and about 1 cm (½ in.) wide.

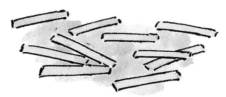

2. From a second color of Bristol board, cut at least ten strips that are 10 cm (4 in.) long and about 1 cm (½ in.) wide.

3. From a third color of Bristol board, cut at least ten strips that are 15 cm (6 in.) long and about 1 cm (½ in.) wide.

4. Use the one-hole punch to make holes at each end of the Bristol board strips.

5. Make some triangles from three strips joined together with the paper fasteners. How many different triangles can you make, without making the same-sized triangle twice?

With these strips, you can make ten different triangles. Three of the triangles are equilateral triangles, with three sides of the same length. These three triangles are similar triangles, which means they have the same shape, although they are different sizes. You can make six different triangles that have two sides of the same length. They are called isosceles triangles. And you can make one triangle with sides of three different lengths. It is called a scalene triangle.

Take a closer look at the three kinds of triangles you just made.

Equilateral triangle
All three sides of this triangle are the same length.

Isosceles triangle
Two sides of this triangle are the same length.

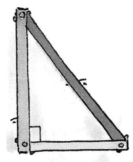

Scalene triangle
The sides of this triangle are all different lengths.

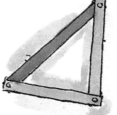

You can't make a triangle from just any three strips of paper. The length of any one side must be shorter than the length of the other two sides added together or it won't work. Check this out for yourself — try making a triangle with two sides of 8 cm (3 in.) and one side of 20 cm (8 in.).

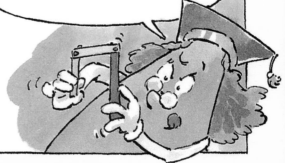

KEEPING IN SHAPE WITH TRIANGLES

You can make shapes with three, four, five, six, sixty or more sides. The triangle is the polygon, or closed flat shape, with the fewest sides. If you tried to make a closed shape with only two sides, all you would get is a V-shape with an open end.

Use your strips of paper and a paper fastener from the last activity (page 67) to make a V-shape. The sides of this V move around like the hands of a clock. But attach a third strip of paper and the sides become locked. Now push on the corners — the triangle keeps its shape. Each side prevents the angle opposite it from opening or closing.

You might think that if three sides are strong, four sides will be even stronger. Try it. Use paper fasteners to attach four strips together. Push on the corners. Hmmm — the four-sided shape squashes flat. What if you add a diagonal strip to the four-sided shape? Now the angles are locked because you have turned your four-sided shape into two triangles.

Do you think more sides will help? Try making a pentagon (a five-sided figure) or a hexagon (six-sided). As you see, adding more sides doesn't help. The triangle is the only polygon that keeps its shape under pressure.

Polygon comes from two Greek words — *poly*, meaning "many," and *gon*, meaning "angles."

THE TRIANGLE UP CLOSE

A **vertex** is a point where two sides of a triangle meet.

An **altitude** is a line from one vertex that is at right angles, or perpendicular, to the opposite side.

The **base** is at the bottom, or lowest side, of a triangle.

The **median** of a triangle is the straight line joining a vertex to a midpoint of the opposite side.

The **midpoint** is the point that divides a side into two equal parts.

You can figure out the distance around the outside of a triangle (its perimeter) by adding up the lengths of its three sides.

FIND THE HIDDEN TRIANGLES

To make this brainteaser, all you need is a square of paper.

1. *Fold the paper in half to make a triangle. Sharpen the crease by running your nail over the fold line.*

2. *Fold the triangle in half, and fold again twice more to end up with a small folded triangle. Sharpen the crease each time.*

3. *When you unfold the paper, you'll see 16 small triangles that are all the same size. How many triangles can you find altogether? (Don't say 16.)* (See page 181 for the answer.)

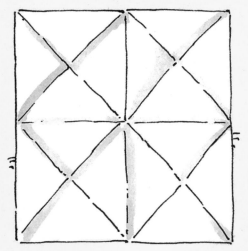

ANGLES

Geese do it when they fly in a V-formation. Trees do it when they branch. Scissors do it when they cut paper. Your arm does it when you bend it to lift something. What are all these things doing? Forming an angle. When two sides come together at one point, they form an angle.

The angles of a triangle come in lots of shapes. Experiment with angles, using the V-shape (two strips of paper joined with a paper fastener) that you made on page 68.

3. Open up the strip a bit more — to look like the hands of a clock set to 12:20 or 12:25 p.m. Now you have an obtuse angle, which is any angle greater than 90° and less than 180°. (An angle of 180° is a straight line and is called a straight angle.)

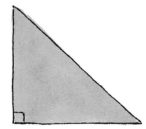

If you sort triangles according to the lengths of their sides, you've already discovered that you get equilateral, isosceles and scalene triangles. But if you sort them according to the sizes of the angles, you get acute triangles, right triangles and obtuse triangles.

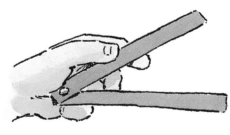

l. Start with the unattached ends close together. This gives you an acute angle — an angle smaller than 90°.

2. Arrange the two strips to look like the two hands of a clock set to 12:15 p.m. — with one hand on the twelve and the other on the three. The angle you have made is a right angle, or a 90° angle.

Acute triangle

Each of the angles measures less than 90°.

Right triangle

Has an angle of 90°.

Obtuse triangle

Has an angle measuring more than 90°.

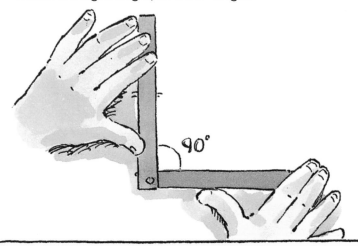

Adding up the angles

What would you call a triangle having both a right angle and an obtuse angle? You'd call it impossible. See for yourself.

You'll need:
- paper
- a pencil
- a ruler
- scissors
- 3 crayons or colored markers of different colors

1. Draw a triangle on the paper and cut it out.

2. Color each angle a different color.

3. Rip off the corners of the triangle.

4. Fit the three corners together around a single point. What do you get?

5. Do you think it was just lucky that you ended up with a straight line? Try it again with a differently shaped triangle.

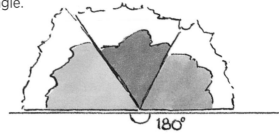

180°

What's happening?
The three angles inside a triangle will always sit together on a straight line. No matter what sizes the three angles are, they always add up to 180°, which is a straight line. That's why you can't have a triangle with both a right angle and an obtuse angle — these angles would add up to more than 180°.

Cutting the angles in half

Cut out a paper triangle and fold one of the angles through its vertex so that the sides touch. When you unfold it, you can see that the fold line now bisects the angle, or divides it into two equal parts. Here's another way to bisect an angle.

You'll need:

- paper
- a pencil
- a ruler
- a compass

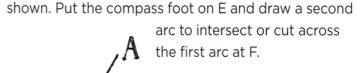

I. Draw any angle ABC with sides at least 8 cm (3 in.) long.

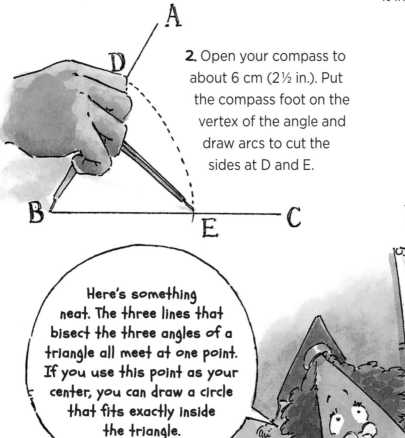

2. Open your compass to about 6 cm (2½ in.). Put the compass foot on the vertex of the angle and draw arcs to cut the sides at D and E.

3. Put the compass foot on D and draw an arc as shown. Put the compass foot on E and draw a second arc to intersect or cut across the first arc at F.

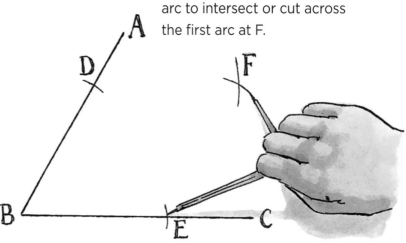

4. The line BF bisects the angle ABC, dividing it in half.

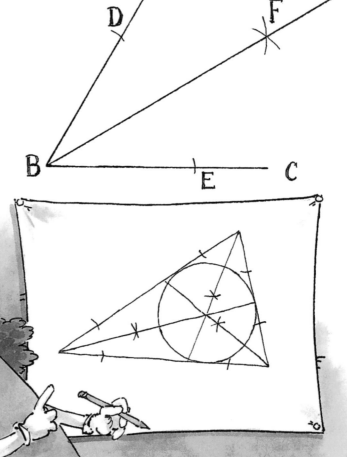

Here's something neat. The three lines that bisect the three angles of a triangle all meet at one point. If you use this point as your center, you can draw a circle that fits exactly inside the triangle.

Area of a triangle

The ancient Egyptians were interested in geometry for a very good reason. Every year the Nile River overflowed and washed away the markers that divided one farmer's field from the next farmer's field. This meant that every year surveyors had to draw new boundaries. To make sure that each farmer got the right amount of land (and paid taxes according to the size of the field), the surveyors had to have an easy way of measuring the area of oddly shaped fields. They did it by marking off the land into big triangles and

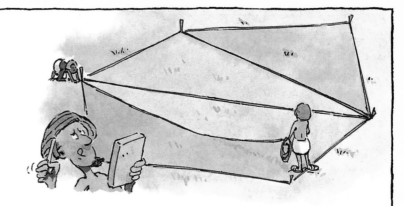

measuring the area of the triangles. They were the first to figure out how much space there is inside a triangle. Here's how to find out the area of a triangle the way the ancient Egyptians did.

You'll need:

- paper
- scissors

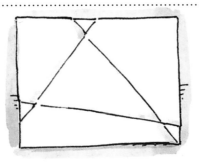

1. Make a triangle by folding three creases in the piece of paper.

2. Cut along the creases. Label the corners of the triangle ABC.

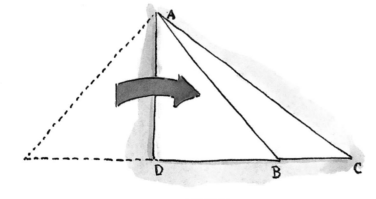

3. Fold through A so that the line BC is folded back along itself. The line you have folded is called an altitude. Label it AD.

4. Fold the triangle again so that A touches D.

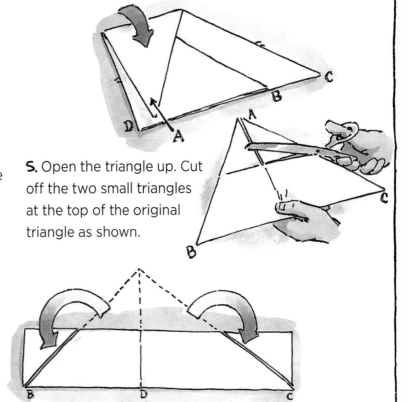

5. Open the triangle up. Cut off the two small triangles at the top of the original triangle as shown.

6. Rearrange the three parts to form rectangles.

The original triangle has the same area as a rectangle, having the same width but only half the height. So the area of a triangle is ½ times the triangle's perpendicular height (or altitude) times its base. For example, if our original triangle had a base of 4 units and an altitude of 6 units, its area would be 12 square units.

Triangular numbers

This may look like a setup for ten-pin bowling, but it's the beginning of a pencil-and-paper game that you can play with a friend. Before you begin, you will need to figure out the trick of the triangular numbers pattern.

You'll need:
- paper
- a pencil

Getting ready

Set up the game board by drawing dots arranged in a triangle — one dot in the first row, two dots in the second row, five dots in the fifth row, ten dots in the tenth row and so on, for as many rows as you like. Of course, the more dots you use, the longer the game will take to finish.

Playing rules
I. Each player takes a turn drawing a line that connects two dots.

2. The point of the game is to draw a line that encloses a triangle. When you enclose a triangle, put your initial inside it.

3. When the last two dots are connected, count up the triangles with your initials. The player with the most triangles wins.

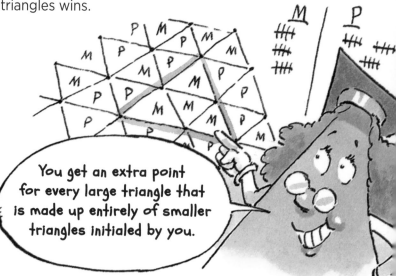

You get an extra point for every large triangle that is made up entirely of smaller triangles initialed by you.

No matter how many rows of dots you draw, the total number of dots will be a triangular number. Triangular numbers are ones that can be arranged as shown to form triangles: 1, 3, 6, 10, 15, 21 and so on. What do you think the next triangular number will be? There is a pattern to triangular numbers. The numbers go up by adding 1, 2, 3, 4, 5 and so on to the previous number. So to get the second triangular number, you add 2 to the first number. To get the third number, you add 3 to the second number and so on. To get the seventh number, you add 7 to the sixth number. That is, you add 7 to 21 to get 28.

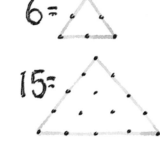

6 =

15 =

PASCAL'S TRIANGLE

You can find triangular numbers, and a lot more, in this arrangement of numbers known as Pascal's triangle. Blaise Pascal was a brilliant French mathematician who lived in the 17th century. When he was only 13, he discovered this triangle, with its very special patterns of numbers. Each number in Pascal's triangle is the sum of the two numbers immediately above it, to the left and right. Can you figure out what the next row of numbers will be? (See page 181 for the answers.)

```
              1
            1   1
          1   2   1
        1   3   3   1
      1   4   6   4   1
    1   5  10  10   5   1
  1   6  15  20  15   6   1
1   7  21  35  35  21   7   1
```

The diagonal column 1, 3, 6, 10, 15, 21 is the series of triangular numbers.

TURN THE TRIANGLE AROUND

A

What is the smallest number of coins that you have to move to change triangle A into triangle B? (See page 181 for the answer.)

B

PHANTOM TRIANGLES

Impossible tri-bar

The 20th-century mathematician Roger Penrose was the first person to draw this tricky triangle on paper, but no one can make a real one in three-dimensional space.

Try it with three pencils. Each angle in this triangle looks like a 90° angle. But three 90° angles add up to 270° — too many degrees to form a triangle (see page 71).

Ghostly triangles

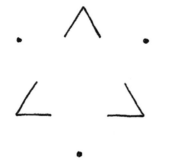

Three dots are enough to give a faint image of a second triangle, covering the gaps of the first one.

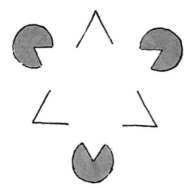

Now the illusory triangle is more obvious.

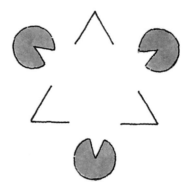

When smaller angles are cut from the circles, the triangle seems to have curved-in sides to account for the gaps.

The Bermuda Triangle

Flashes of light from the sky, compasses spinning around wildly, ghost ships, lost crews, unexplained engine failures and wrecked planes. It sounds like a mystery movie, but some people think this is what you'll find if you venture into the Bermuda Triangle. This mysterious triangle is the part of the Atlantic Ocean enclosed by lines joining the tips of Florida, Bermuda and Puerto Rico. Some people claim that an unknown force in this triangular area strikes down ships and airplanes and sinks them without a trace. However, many people believe that the accidents are all caused by bad weather and human error.

Triangle takeaway

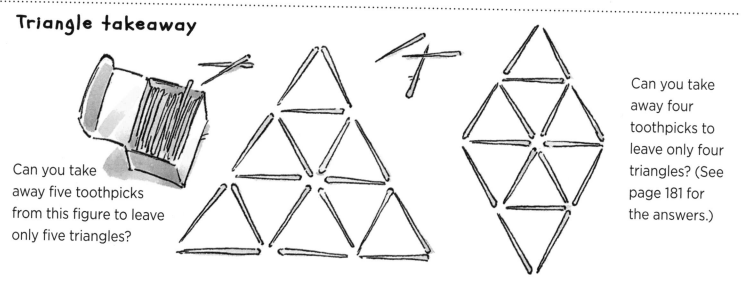

Can you take away five toothpicks from this figure to leave only five triangles?

Can you take away four toothpicks to leave only four triangles? (See page 181 for the answers.)

2. SPECIAL TRIANGLES

Ask a friend to draw a triangle. Chances are your friend won't draw just any triangle but one of these three special models: the right triangle, the isosceles triangle or the equilateral triangle. Read on to find out why these three are old favorites.

RIGHT TRIANGLES

Start with a square of paper, fold it in half along the diagonal, and you get a right-angled triangle. This triangle is one of the most important of all. It helped the Egyptians build the base of their pyramids and it is the shape for sails that move sailboats across the waves. It's even useful for measuring the height of tall trees or buildings. What makes this triangle special is the right angle that gives the triangle its name. A square corner, such as the corner of this book, is a right angle.

Ancient geometry

Egyptians didn't have fancy drafting tools, but they were able to make perfect right angles every time for the bases of their pyramids. The Egyptians used ropes with knots tied at equal intervals to make their measurements. It took three rope-stretchers to make the angle. Check this out for yourself. You can use black marks instead of knots if you like.

You'll need:

- a piece of string about 1 m (3 ft.) long
- a measuring stick
- a black marker
- scissors
- a friend

1. Ask someone to hold the string tight along the measuring stick. Starting at one end of the string, make marks with your black marker every 5 cm (2 in.) along the string until you have made 12 equally spaced marks. Cut the string on the twelfth mark. The remaining 11 marks divide the string into 12 equal units.

2. Ask your rope-stretcher to hold together the two ends of the string. Call this point A.

3. Count along the string until you find a mark 3 units away from A. Hold this part of the string in one hand and tighten it to make one side of the triangle.

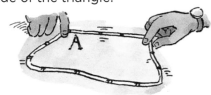

4. Count along the string 5 more units. Hold this part of the string in your other hand.

5. Pull the triangle tight. You should now have a triangle with sides 3, 4 and 5 units long — count them. Check that you really have a right angle by matching it against the corner of this book. (In a triangle, the right angle is always the one across from the longest side, which is called the hypotenuse.)

What's happening?

The ancient Greek mathematician Pythagoras showed why a triangle with sides of 3, 4, and 5 units long will always contain a right angle. It's because of the way the lengths of the sides are related to one another. Pythagoras discovered a relationship that holds true for all right triangles. In what is now known as the Pythagorean theorem, Pythagoras proved that the square formed on the hypotenuse (the side opposite the right angle) has the same area as the sum of the squares formed on the other two sides.

In this triangle with sides of 3, 4 and 5 units, the square on the hypotenuse is 5^2 or $5 \times 5 = 25$ square units. Count the squares on the other two sides to see if they add up to 25.

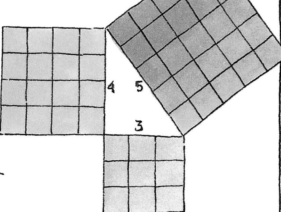

MEASURING HEIGHT

Thales, the first known Greek mathematician, traveled to Egypt and amazed the Pharaoh by figuring out the height of the Great Pyramid, which rose 147 m (481 ft.) above its square base with 230-m (755-ft.) long sides. How did he do it? By using similar right-angled triangles. Similar triangles have exactly the same shape, even if they're not the same size. If you photocopied a triangle using the reducing button that shrinks a picture to half its size, you would end up with similar triangles. The sides of the copied triangle would be only half as long as the sides of the original triangle, but the angles would be all the same.

To measure the height of the Great Pyramid, Thales also made a smaller model of the original. At the time of day when his own shadow was the same length as his height, he measured the Great Pyramid's shadow. Since he cast a shadow as long as his own height, Thales realized that the pyramid's shadow at that time of day must also equal its height. So to find the pyramid's height, all he had to do was measure the length of its shadow. The similar-triangle method is a great way to measure anything that is tricky to measure directly — such as a tree, a waterfall or a tall building.

Thales had to include in his measurement the distance from the pyramid's outside wall to the center of the pyramid below its highest point.

ISOSCELES TRIANGLES

Fold a piece of notepaper in half, and cut along the diagonal as shown. Unfold the paper and you have an isosceles triangle. You know that the two sides of this triangle are the same length because you just cut them out with one cut. But you might not have noticed that the angles at the base of this triangle are also the same size. The isosceles triangle has mirror symmetry — it's exactly the same on one side of the fold line as it is on the other. So two sides and two angles are exactly the same.

The isosceles triangle is a good shape for paper airplanes, darts and arrowheads. Its mirror symmetry makes each side perfectly balanced so that it flies straight. The pointy tip makes the shape streamlined and reduces air resistance. Hunters as far back as 4000 years ago used flint arrowheads that looked like isosceles triangles. Some birds and fish have also adopted a dart shape to help them speed through air and water.

70°

70°

Paper airplane math

All proper darts are symmetrical, like isosceles triangles: every fold you make on one side of the center fold you also have to make on the other. Put this paper airplane to a flight test: what's your record for distance traveled and time spent in the air?

You'll need:

- a piece of notepaper 21.6 × 28 cm (8½ × 11 in.)
- a pencil
- a ruler
- sticky tape

1. Fold the notepaper in half with the long sides together.

2. Open up the paper. Draw some lines on the paper as shown, to tell where to fold the airplane. First draw a line 10 cm (4 in.) from the top edge of the paper.

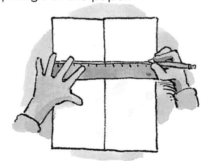

3. Draw two lines 0.5 cm (¼ in.) on either side of the center fold.

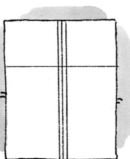

4. Make two marks at the bottom of the paper 4 cm (1½ in.) from the center fold. Starting at the top of the center fold, draw diagonal lines to these two marks.

5. In the squares at the top of the paper, fold two right-angled triangles.

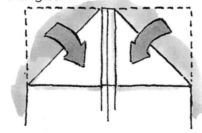

6. Fold again as shown so that the fold lines from step 5 touch the lines on either side of the middle fold.

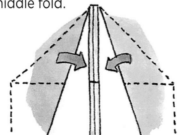

7. Fold the paper along the middle line, so the folded parts are on the outside. Sharpen the crease by running your thumbnail over the fold line and unfold.

8. Now for the last step. On each side, fold along the diagonal line that you drew in step 4.

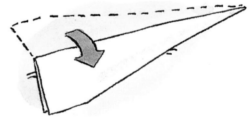

9. Hold the wings together underneath with some sticky tape. Use some sticky tape on the top to make the wings tilt slightly upwards. Now you're ready to fly.

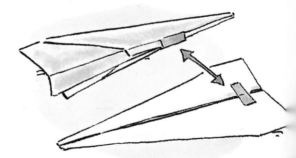

SURVEYING BY TRIANGULATION

Without the triangle, engineers could never have bored the Simplon Tunnel through the mountains of the Alps in 1906. This tunnel connecting Switzerland and Italy is 20 km (12 mi.) long. Workers started drilling from both sides of the mountain. When the two parts of the tunnel met in the middle of the mountain, they missed a perfect alignment by only 10 cm (4 in.). The surveyors had set up the drilling machines to cut along the 10-km (6-mi.) sides of two very big triangles. Surveying by triangulation is based on a simple fact about a triangle. If one side and two angles of a triangle are known, the other two sides and remaining angle can be figured out easily.

You don't need to be a surveyor to use triangles for measuring distances. Every time you reach out to grab something, you use the same principle of triangulation. The triangle used here is the isosceles triangle made by your two eyes and the object your eyes are focusing on. To check this out, you'll need a friend to help out and a pen with a removable top.

1. Remove the top from the pen and hold on to the top. Give the pen to your friend. Now sit across a table from your friend and close your eyes.

2. Ask your friend to hold the pen straight up and down, about 60 cm (24 in.) in front of you.

3. Open only one eye. Try to put the top on the pen.

4. Open both eyes. How close were you? If you missed, try again, this time with both eyes open.

What's happening?

Why do you need two eyes to figure out how far away something is? The answer lies in the triangle. If you know the length of one side — the base line — and the size of the angles on this line, you can find all three points of any triangle. In this pen experiment, you know the base line, which is the distance between your own eyes. When the muscles in your eyes contract to focus on the pen, your brain uses this information to figure out the angles on the base line. Knowing the length of the base line and the size of the two angles on the base line, your brain can calculate how far away the third point of the triangle is — the pen. But close one eye and now you know only the base line and one angle, which is not enough to reconstruct the whole triangle. Surveyors calculate distances the same way — by knowing the length of a base line and the size of the angles on the base line.

Triangle trees

Cut an isosceles triangle into a lacy tree for decorating gift boxes or hanging on your Christmas tree.

You'll need:
- a square of colored paper
- scissors

1. Fold the square of paper in half diagonally.

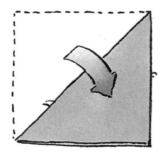

2. Fold it in half again as shown. Fold it a third time to end up with a long, narrow triangle.

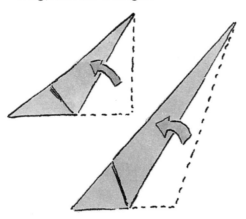

3. Trim the bottom to make the folded sides the same length. Now you have an isosceles triangle.

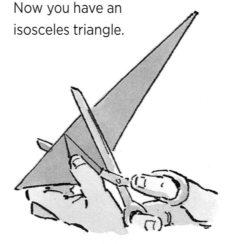

4. Make cuts about 1 cm (½ in.) apart all along one fold line. Don't cut all the way across, but leave some paper uncut at the other fold line.

5. Similarly, on the second fold line, make cuts in between the first cuts.

6. Unfold the paper. Carefully pull on the top and bottom of the triangle to open it up into a lacy, decorative triangle tree.

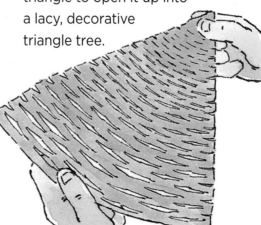

EQUILATERAL TRIANGLES

The isosceles triangle has one line of symmetry (the fold line formed when you match the two equal sides together), but the equilateral triangle has three lines of symmetry. Because it has three equal sides and three equal angles, you can fold an equilateral triangle exactly in half in three different ways. An equilateral triangle is the shape of the three-leaf clover, the trillium and the iris, which also all have three lines of symmetry. In many different civilizations, people have made designs like those you see here, based on the three-fold symmetry of the equilateral triangle.

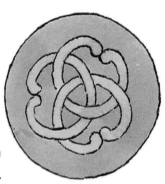

Traditional Japanese design

Spiral of life — ancient Irish symbol

Modern symbol for wool products

12

12

12

Equilateral designs

Starting with an equilateral triangle, you can cut out some intricate designs and see three-fold symmetry at work.

You'll need:

- a square of paper
- a plastic triangle used for drafting. (If you don't have a drafter's triangle, see "Fold an equilateral triangle" on page 87.)
- scissors
- a pencil

Use this vertex to draw the 60° angle.

I. Fold the square in half along the diagonal. Sharpen the crease by running your thumbnail over the fold line.

2. Find the center of the fold line by folding it in half. Mark the midpoint with a dot.

3. Line up the short side of the plastic triangle along the fold line, with the 60° vertex on the dot. Draw a line as shown. Fold along the line and sharpen the crease.

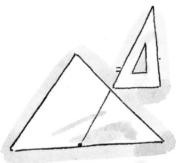

4. Fold the other side over. Sharpen the crease line.

5. Turn the paper over. Cut off the uneven edges to get an equilateral triangle.

6. Unfold the paper — you should have a hexagon, made from six equilateral triangles.

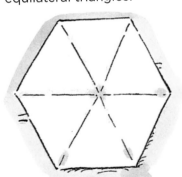

7. To get a fancier design, fold the paper back into the triangle of step 5.

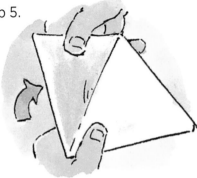

8. Use your pencil to outline a design. Here are some shapes to try, or you can invent your own.

9. Unfold the paper. Because of the way you folded the paper, all your patterns will have a single design element that is repeated six times — three times as your original design, and three times as the mirror image of your design.

FOLD AN EQUILATERAL TRIANGLE

If you don't have a plastic triangle handy for measuring the 60° angle needed for the equilateral triangle designs, it's no problem. This folding trick gives you an equilateral triangle, which means you'll have three perfect 60° angles every time.

You'll need:
- notepaper
- a pencil

1. Label the corners of the piece of notepaper ABCD as shown.

2. Fold the paper in half, long sides together, so that AB touches CD. Unfold the paper.

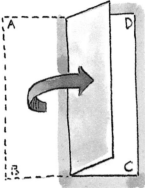

3. Fold the short side BC so that C touches the fold line.

4. With the folded side as the base, fold the right side down so that the edge of the paper is lined up along the base.

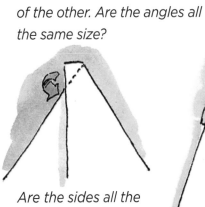

5. Fold the extra paper on the left side under as shown. Check to see that you really have an equilateral triangle. Match the angles by placing them one on top of the other. Are the angles all the same size?

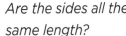

Are the sides all the same length?

To make a hexagon, or six-sided shape, fold in the corners of the equilateral triangle so that they meet in the center of the triangle.

Triangle weave

The triangle spider is an expert in weaving triangular webs. But you don't need to be a triangle spider to weave this amazing design. Start with an equilateral triangle, and turn some straight lines into curves.

You'll need:
- a square of stiff cardboard with sides at least 22 cm (9 in.) long. (Cardboard must be stiff or it won't lie flat when the threads are woven.)
- a ruler
- a plastic triangle or a compass
- a pencil
- scissors
- 3 colors of thread, each about 2.7 m (9 ft.) long. Use colors that contrast well with the cardboard.

Draw an equilateral triangle

1. Near the bottom of the square of cardboard, draw a line 20 cm (8 in.) long, parallel to the edge. This line will be the base of an equilateral triangle.

2. Use the plastic triangle to construct a 60° angle at one end of the base line. (If you don't have a plastic triangle handy, use your compass to construct a small equilateral triangle at one end of the base. See "Dissection puzzle" on page 90 to find out how.

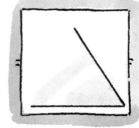

3. Extend the second line to make it 20 cm (8 in.) long.

4. Draw the third side. Check with your ruler to make sure that this third side is also 20 cm (8 in.) long.

Prepare the triangle for weaving

5. Use a ruler and pencil to mark the sides every 1 cm (½ in.). You should have 19 marks on each side (15 if you are using inches).

6. Cut out the triangle.

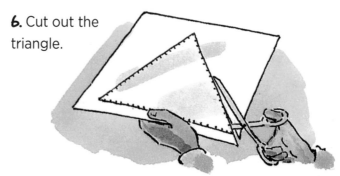

7. At each mark, make a short cut at right angles to the sides of the triangle. Then make a short cut at each of the three vertices. These cuts are the slots that will hold the thread when you are weaving.

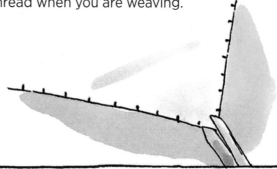

Weave some curves

8. This is the tricky part. But numbering the slots on the back of the cardboard will help you put the threads in the right place. Start at a vertex and number each cut along one side from 1 up to 20 (16 if you are working in inches). Number the slots on the other side of the same vertex by working back from 20 (or 16) to 1.

9. Cut a piece of thread that is about 2.7 m (9 ft.) long. Pull the thread up through slot 1 at the vertex. Leave about 10 cm (4 in.) of thread as a tail to tie up later. Stretch the long end of the thread across the front of the triangle to slot 1 on the other side. On the back, stretch the thread to slot 2 and pull it through.

10. On the front, stretch the thread to the opposite side to slot 2. Keep weaving the thread from side to side as shown. If you are putting the thread in the right slots, the back of the triangle will look like this. When you get to the last slot and have completed the curve, pull the thread to the back and tie it to the other end of the thread.

11. Weave the other two curves in the same way.

REULEAUX TRIANGLE

At the center of your triangle weave, you will see an interesting shape, called a Reuleaux triangle, which is far more useful than it looks. What makes it special is that, like a circle, the Reuleaux triangle is a curve of constant width. The Philadelphia Fire Department has used this shape since the 1950s for the fire hydrant shaft that controls the water. This way they keep their fire hydrants safe from pranksters who want to chill out in the summer heat. Viewed from the top, the fire hydrant shaft looks like an equilateral triangle with curved sides. Since the Reuleaux triangle is a curve of constant width, the parallel jaws of an ordinary wrench slip around and around it, the way they would around a circle. This makes it difficult, or impossible, for most people to turn them. (Firefighters carry their own specially shaped wrenches to turn on the water.)

Dissection puzzle

This dissection puzzle is like Humpty Dumpty — a lot easier to take apart than it is to put together again. Once you've made the puzzle, challenge a friend to put it together.

You'll need:

• Bristol board or cardboard (it's best to use something that is the same color on both sides — it makes the puzzles trickier to solve)
• a pencil
• a ruler
• a compass
• scissors
• paper

I. You're going to draw an equilateral triangle on the Bristol board. Start by drawing the base. A base of 8 cm (3 in.) works well.

2. Put the compass foot on one end of the base line and draw an arc above the line as shown, keeping the compass opening the same distance apart as the length of the base.

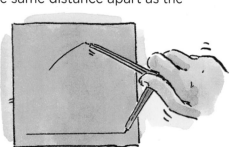

3. Put the compass foot on the other end of the line and draw a second arc to intersect the first arc. This intersection point is the third vertex of the triangle. Draw the other two sides of the triangle.

4. Cut out the triangle.

5. Before you cut out the puzzle, draw a diagram of the cuts you plan to make. Here are examples of some four-piece puzzles and some six-piece puzzles, but let your imagination go wild and design your own.

6. Cut out the puzzle. The puzzle you designed may be so tricky that even you can't put the pieces back together! But you can always consult your diagram if you're stumped.

Triangle fractals

Mathematicians call these strange shapes "fractals." Each part of the design is a miniature of the whole design. You can find fractals in nature if you look carefully at a

cross section of broccoli or cauliflower. See how each small part is a tiny version of the whole thing. An ordinary equilateral triangle is the starting point for both of the fractals shown here.

You'll need:
- white paper
- a pencil
- a ruler
- a compass
- a black marker

The Sierpinski gasket

A Sierpinski gasket is a fractal formed by taking away the small triangle formed when you bisect the sides of an equilateral triangle and connect the midpoints.

I. Draw an equilateral triangle.

2. Bisect the sides.

3. Draw lines connecting the midpoints of the sides to form four smaller triangles.

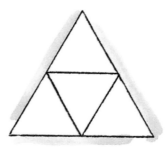

4. Leave the middle triangle alone. Repeat steps 2 and 3 with the other three triangles. Repeat as many times as you like.

5. Leave the middle triangles white, and color the others black, as shown. Each time you remove small triangles from the center, you have less and less black space in the design. Eventually you would end up with all white space.

Koch snowflake

For this fractal you don't take away triangles; you add them. You make a Koch snowflake by adding small equilateral triangles to the sides of larger triangles. After a few steps, you get a lacy snowflake.

I. Draw an equilateral triangle with sides of 15 cm (6 in.).

2. Measure the sides and divide them exactly into three equal sections.

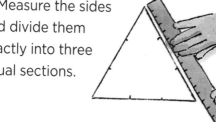

3. Make a smaller equilateral triangle on the middle section of the sides.

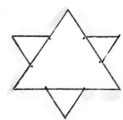

4. Continue as before. Divide the sides of the smaller triangles in three and construct a smaller equilateral triangle on the middle section of the sides.

5. Repeat as many times as you like. With each step, you make the perimeter around the outside of the triangle longer.

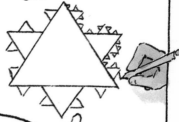

This shape was named after Helge von Koch, who first discovered it in 1904 when he was studying curves.

Hexaflexagon

Transform a chain of equilateral triangles into a puzzle that flips and twists itself inside out.

You'll need:

- yellow or white Bristol board
- a pencil
- a ruler
- a plastic triangle with a 60° angle
- scissors
- glue
- 2 contrasting colors of poster paint and a paintbrush

1. Measure and cut a strip of Bristol board that is about 5 cm by 35 cm (2 in. by 14 in.). A smaller or larger strip is fine — just cut your strip seven times as long as it is wide.

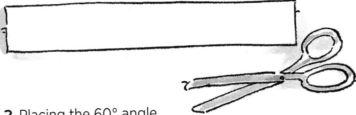

2. Placing the 60° angle on the strip as shown, draw a line to the top of the strip. This line is the first side of an equilateral triangle.

3. Placing the 60° angle along this line, draw a second line to complete the triangle.

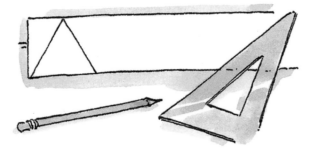

4. Draw nine more triangles the same way.

5. Trim off the ends to leave a strip of triangles.

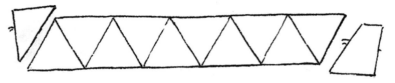

6. Use the point of the compass to score the zigzag lines. This will make the cardboard easier to fold. Fold back and forth along each fold line.

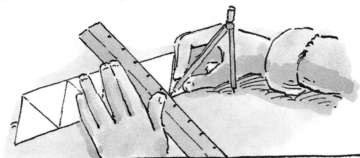

Tetrahedron

Square pyramid

Octahedron

Petal shape

Before you fold and glue the strip into a hexaflexagon, experiment with making these three-dimensional shapes. Check out how many triangles meet at one vertex.

7. Lay out the strip as shown and number the triangles.

8. Flip the strip over and label the triangles on the back. Make sure that triangle 11 is the back of triangle 1.

9. To fold the hexaflexagon, hold the strip as shown and fold triangle 11 over triangle 12. Then fold triangle 15 on triangle 14. Fold triangle 8 on triangle 7.

10. Glue triangle 10 to triangle 1. (If you end up with a different arrangement, you have folded it wrong and should try again.)

11. When the glue is dry, carefully paint each side of the hexaflexagon a different color and let dry.

12. Gently twist the hexaflexagon along the folds until it flattens into a different color pattern. How many different patterns can you find?

What's an octopus?

An eight-sided cat.

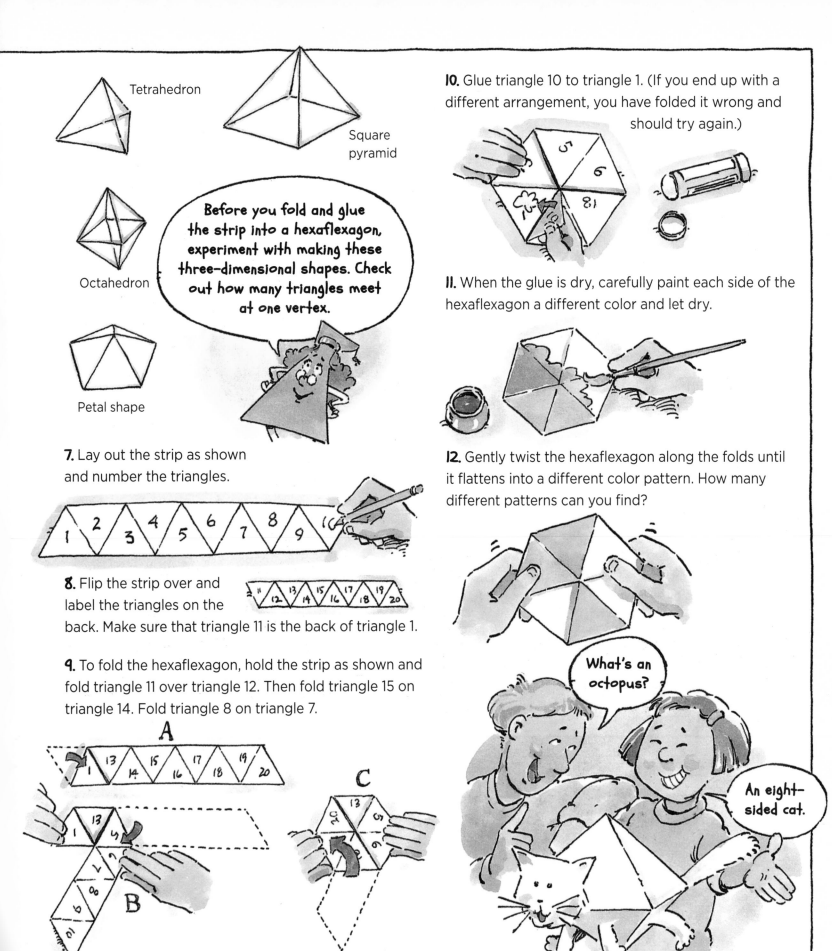

93

3. BUILDING WITH TRIANGLES

If you were on a moving train or ferryboat, how would you stand to keep your balance? If you stood with your legs apart, you'd be turning yourself into a human triangle. Triangles are stable and strong. That's why builders and architects use them for lightweight bridges and towers. As you have seen, you can push a square out of shape by pinching its corners together, but you can't squash a triangle. The only structure that holds its shape under pressure is a triangle.

Look around you. Can you find examples of triangles that make things strong? You probably didn't think of the hidden triangle in a slice of green pepper. Since the green pepper is almost hollow inside, it's much lighter than a solid fruit of the same size, such as an orange. The green pepper keeps its firm, rounded shape because of its inner triangular ribs.

How about a shelf support, an ironing board, a window fastening holding a window open, a bicycle frame, a deck chair, a gate or the timbers in the roof? Triangles strengthen hydro towers and the crossarms of telephone poles. The long boom of a building crane is made of relatively thin pieces of steel, but its triangular shape makes it strong enough to hoist heavy machines to the top of a high-rise building. Triangles are strong and rigid because of one key fact: a triangle can't change its shape unless one of its sides gets longer or shorter.

Putting triangles to work

Take a piece of paper and hold it at the corners along one edge. See how it droops — it can't support even its own weight. So how could you make it stronger? You could glue some cardboard stiffeners along its length. But you don't need anything that fancy — just some triangles. Try this strength test.

You'll need:
- paper
- 2 boxes
- some paperback books

I. Fold the paper into a fan.

2. Support the ends of the fan on two boxes to make a bridge structure.

3. Test the strength of your bridge by putting a paperback book on it. Keep adding books until the bridge breaks.

What's happening?

The same piece of paper that couldn't support even itself can now hold the weight of several books. You've made the original paper at least 300 times stronger by folding it into triangles. Triangles are also what make corrugated cardboard strong enough to use for cartons for packing groceries. If you cut into a piece of corrugated cardboard, you will see an inside layer of triangular folds sandwiched between the two outer layers of paper.

Bridges

Building a bridge over a small stream is a snap. Put some planks across the stream and you're ready to go. But what if the stream is too wide for the plank to reach across? Try this bridge-building experiment, using only cardboard strips and paper fasteners. Test out different ways to connect the strips together to make a section at least 30 cm (12 in.) long.

You'll need:

- Bristol board
- a ruler
- a pencil
- scissors
- a one-hole punch
- a package of paper fasteners

1. Cut out 15 strips of Bristol board that are 10 cm (4 in.) long and 1 cm (½ in.) wide. (You can reuse the cardboard strips from "Making triangles," page 67.)

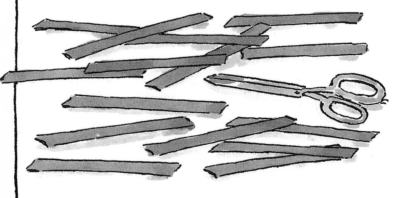

2. Punch holes at each end of the Bristol board strips.

3. Use the strips and paper fasteners to make a bridge at least 30 cm (12 in.) long.

Put your bridge to the test by using it to span two stacks of books set 20 cm (8 in.) apart.

If you used triangles to build your bridge, you get an A+ in engineering skills. As you can see, you don't need long pieces of building material to span a wide gap. Short ones will work as long as they are locked together into triangles, as they are in the famous bridges shown on the next two pages.

RAILWAY BRIDGES

The bridge you built from cardboard strips is actually called a truss and looks like the railway trusses built in North America more than a hundred years ago during the great age of trains. Thousands of new bridges were built to span the deep gorges and wild rivers of the continent. The problem is that the longer a bridge is, the heavier it gets. If it is very long, it can break under its own weight. A bridge builder can always reduce a bridge's weight by using less building material. But since the bridge has to be strong enough to support the extra weight of a thundering train, the bridge builder doesn't want to reduce weight at the expense of strength or rigidity.

The solution is to cut away all the material not actually needed to give the bridge strength. When all the inessential material is cut away, you are left with open structures that are light because they are full of holes, or meshes. Strength and rigidity come from the design miracle — the triangle. This airy bridge of triangles was built in 1901 over the Dead Horse Gulch near the White Pass in British Columbia, Canada.

These patterns aren't string games; they're different trusses patented during the railway era and named after their inventors. Zigzag crossbars connect the parallel bars on the top and bottom to form N-shapes, M-shapes or W-shapes — they all work as long as they form the chain of triangles needed for strength and rigidity.

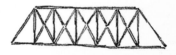

Howe truss

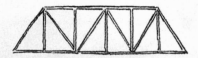

Baltimore truss

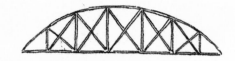

Whipple bowstring truss

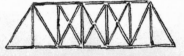

Pratt truss

Warren truss

Bollman truss

The Firth of Forth Bridge in Scotland (shown here), completed in 1890 with a span of 529 m (1735 ft.), is still one of the great bridges of the world.

MONUMENTS

The Eiffel Tower

Before he designed the Eiffel Tower for the Paris Exhibition of 1889, Gustave Eiffel had already built many iron viaducts and bridges and had learned a lot about using triangulated structures to resist the blows of wind and water. Nevertheless, for his tower, he didn't leave anything to chance. Before starting the building, he made over 5000 drawings of all parts of the tower, drawings that called for 15 000 structural pieces and 2 500 000 rivet holes.

At 300 m (986 ft.), his wrought-iron tower rose almost twice as high as the 1884 Washington Monument, till then the world's tallest structure.

The Eiffel Tower weighs about 6350 t (7000 tn.) — if you think that sounds heavy, compare it to the Washington Monument's 89 000 t (98 000 tn.) of stone. The Washington Monument gets its strength from the sheer weight of its piled stone, but the Eiffel Tower is strong through good design. Like the truss, the Eiffel Tower is mostly air and a lacy frame of triangles. If you melted its frame down, it would form a block about 5 cm (2 in.) thick that would fit under its own four legs.

Although in the beginning some people complained that the Eiffel Tower "stood up from Paris like a hatpin," now it's the most famous building in France.

Giant egg

To celebrate the 100th anniversary of the Royal Canadian Mounted Police in 1974, the Alberta government offered grants for community projects. A giant statue of a Mountie, a maple leaf or some other standard Canadian symbol was not good enough for the town of Vegreville, Alberta. Vegreville proposed to build a 3½-story-high Ukrainian Easter egg, or Pysanka, to honor the Ukrainian pioneers who had settled the area.

Who could they get to build an egg 10 m (31 ft.) high? Finally Ronald Resch, a computer science professor from the University of Utah, took on the job. For the movie *Star Trek*, he had designed the futuristic mouth of a spaceship that swallowed up everything in its path. Resch's plan for the egg was to make it using many flat tiles joined together at slight angles.

So what shape should the tiles be? It's cheaper to produce tiles if they can all be made the same shape. There are only three regular shapes that will cover a flat surface without overlapping or leaving gaps — the square, the hexagon and the equilateral triangle. Resch discovered that he could tile the egg with 1108 same-sized, equilateral triangles if he interspersed them with 524 three-pointed stars.

How well has this egg survived wind, water and gravity? After all, Humpty Dumpty had problems. "We've had no trouble with the Pysanka in any way," said Vegreville's mayor. "The structure was made to last." The egg sits serenely on its base of concrete and steel and turns in the wind like a weather vane.

BUILDINGS

Did you know that triangles brace high-rise buildings against the wind so that people on the top floor don't get dizzy? In some steel skyscrapers, the elevator shaft at the center is surrounded by a cage made of four triangulated frames that run all the way from the bottom right up to the top of the building. These Xed-frames are actually trusses, with the same qualities of lightness and strength.

Usually the Xed-frame is hidden at the building's core, but in the John Hancock Insurance Company Building in Chicago, the frame of triangles was put on the outside. Smart real estate agents charge more rent to the two offices on each floor that have a window blocked by the diagonal frame — they say it's a status symbol.

Sydney Opera House

The Danish architect Jørn Utzon never really expected to win the 1957 competition to design the Sydney Opera House in Australia. In fact, when people first looked at his design, they said it was weird and not very useful. His plans called for a series of ten concrete vaults, like big triangular sails, up to 60 m (200 ft.) high, rising one behind the other. Utzon came up with the triangular shapes for his vaults by slicing different segments out of three wooden balls. The building was opened as a performing arts center in 1973 and has become a famous landmark. Rising above Sydney Harbour, it suggests water, waves and sails.

ROOFS

Triangles are a clue to weather and climate. To see how, fold a piece of paper in half and set it on the table as shown. Quebec farmhouses and Swiss chalets need roofs this steep so that the snow will slide off. Open up the sides of the paper a bit, and you get a gentle slope suited to climates with rain but not much snow. Flatten the paper right out, and you get a roof suitable for Mexico or the Mediterranean, where it is hot and dry. From this map showing roof slopes, you can figure out which places are cold and snowy, which places have rain but not much snow, which places are hot with lots of rain and which places are dry and hot.

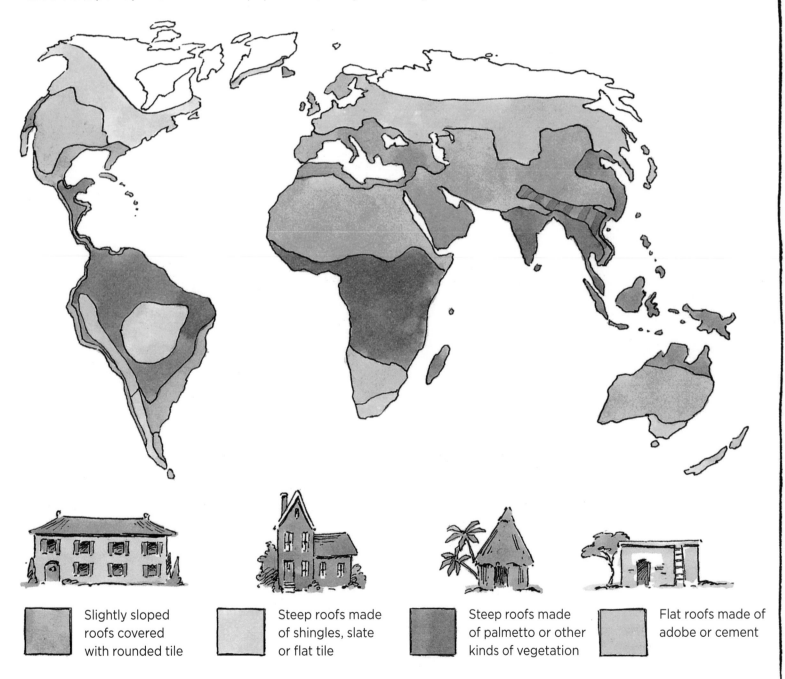

Slightly sloped roofs covered with rounded tile

Steep roofs made of shingles, slate or flat tile

Steep roofs made of palmetto or other kinds of vegetation

Flat roofs made of adobe or cement

4. TRIANGULAR PRISM

When you think of a prism, you may think of a piece of glass that breaks up the sunlight into rainbow colors. But the word "prism" really refers to a shape. A prism is a solid figure. A prism must have a base and a top that are parallel and the same size and shape, and the sides of a prism must be parallelograms. The secret to identifying a prism is counting the number of sides in the prism's base — three sides make a triangular prism, four sides make a rectangular prism, five sides make a pentagonal prism, six sides make a hexagonal prism (the shape bees use for the cells in their honeycombs) and twenty sides make a twenty-sided prism.

Mathematicians call this a net for making a triangular prism. It uses an equilateral triangle, so the rectangular sides are all the same width. But you can make a prism from any kind of triangle, including scalene triangles.

A parallelogram is a four-sided shape with opposite sides that are parallel.

If you set a triangular prism down on one of its rectangular faces, you have a shape like an A-frame house, which does a great job of keeping snow off the roof. If you flatten out the triangular face, you get a wedge shape, which is the shape of an ax.

If oranges could be grown in the shape of triangular prisms, fruit growers could pack them together to fill up all the space in the crate, without leaving any gaps or air holes in between.

Make your own kaleidoscope

The kaleidoscope was invented around 1816, and it's been a hit ever since. With this prism-shaped toy, you can produce new symmetrical designs with a flick of the wrist.

You'll need:

- 3 small mirrors (not round ones) that are all the same size (you can get them in a drugstore)
- masking tape
- a pencil
- a small piece of stiff, clear plastic (e.g., the kind you find as baked-goods covers in grocery stores)
- scissors
- a small piece of waxed paper
- paper of different colors

I. Tape the three small mirrors together as shown to form the sides of a triangular prism.

Before you go further, discover how reflections in the three mirrors work to create patterns. Draw a large comma shape like this  on a piece of paper. Put the prism over top of the paper so that the comma shape is near one of the vertices. How many reflections do you get? Are all reflections the same?

2. Trace the base of the triangular prism on the clear plastic sheet, and cut out the triangle. Repeat this step to get a second clear plastic triangle.

3. Trace the base of the triangular prism on wax paper, and cut out the triangle.

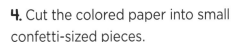

4. Cut the colored paper into small confetti-sized pieces.

5. Put tape along the edges of one plastic triangle so that half the tape sticks out as shown.

6. Make a sandwich of triangles. Start with the taped plastic triangle (make sure the sticky side is facing up). Cover the triangle with the piece of wax paper. Add the small pieces of colored paper. Cover with the second plastic triangle.

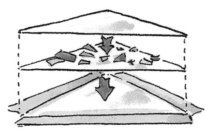

7. Put the prism over the triangle sandwich and secure the tape.

8. Hold the kaleidoscope up to your eye and look toward a light source (but don't look directly into the sun). The pattern of colored paper is reflected six times to make an intricate design. Shake the kaleidoscope each time you want another pattern.

Make a construction kit

With this construction kit, you can make prisms and lots more shapes, too. If you have enough construction units, you can make octet trusses, twisty shapes and even wheels.

Just make sure that the sides of the construction units are all the same length so that the squares and triangles fit together.

You'll need:

- Bristol board or cardboard
- a pencil
- a ruler
- a compass
- scissors
- a one-hole punch
- a box of 5-cm (2-in.) elastics

I. Draw an equilateral triangle with sides 10 cm (4 in.) long (see "Dissection puzzle" on page 90 for instructions). Use the pointed end of the compass to score the lines outlining the triangle.

2. Draw a slightly larger triangle as a 0.5 cm (¼ in.) frame around the first one. Cut out the larger triangle.

3. Punch a hole at each vertex of the small triangle. Trim the corners and fold up the edges along the score lines.

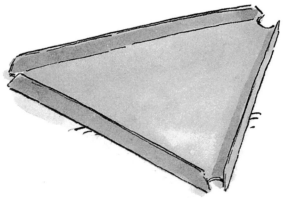

4. You need at least one additional triangle for the prism. Make more triangular units the same way. (With 20 triangles, you can go wild and make an icosahedron.)

5. Now make a square unit. Draw a square with sides 10 cm (4 in.) long. Use the pointed end of the compass to score the lines outlining the square.

6. Draw a slightly larger square as a 0.5 cm (¼ in.) frame around the first one. Cut out the larger square.

7. Punch a hole at each corner of the small square. Trim the corners and fold up the edges along the score lines.

8. You need at least two more square units for the prism. Make more square units the same way.

9. To make a prism, start by lining up two squares as shown to form an edge. Join them by fitting an elastic over the punched holes.

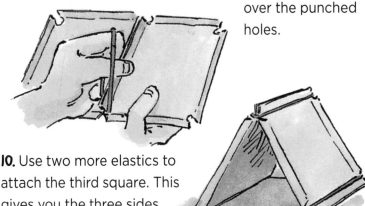

10. Use two more elastics to attach the third square. This gives you the three sides of the triangular prism.

11. With three elastics, attach one triangle to form a top.

12. With three more elastics, attach the second triangle to form a base and complete the prism.

13. When you are finished with your construction, remove the elastics and recycle the building units for other structures. You can store the building units in a big plastic ice cream container.

The equilateral triangle and the square are both regular polygons. In a regular polygon, all the sides are the same length and all the angles are equal.

PLATONIC SOLIDS

You can use your construction kit from page 104 to make some neat shapes called Platonic solids. Sound like something from outer space? Well, the Platonic solids are simply shapes, but they all have two things in common. First, they have faces that are congruent, regular polygons. This means that each face in a Platonic solid has equal angles as well as sides that are the same length (like the square and the equilateral triangle you just made), and each face is the same size and shape. Second, the same number of faces must meet at each vertex. The Platonic solids are the only five shapes possible that meet these requirements, and you can make four of them with your construction kit.

Icosahedron

Use 20 equilateral triangles. Fit 5 triangles around each vertex.

Tetrahedron

Use 4 equilateral triangles. Fit 3 triangles around each vertex.

Cube

Use 6 square units. Fit 3 around each vertex.

Octahedron

Use 8 equilateral triangles. Fit 4 triangles around each vertex.

Dodecahedron

To make the fifth Platonic solid, you need regular pentagons, which have five sides all the same length. Use 12 pentagonal units. Fit 3 pentagons around each vertex.

IT MUST BE A SIGN

Triangles can mean many things, depending on who is reading the signs. Here are some of the meanings that triangles have for different people:

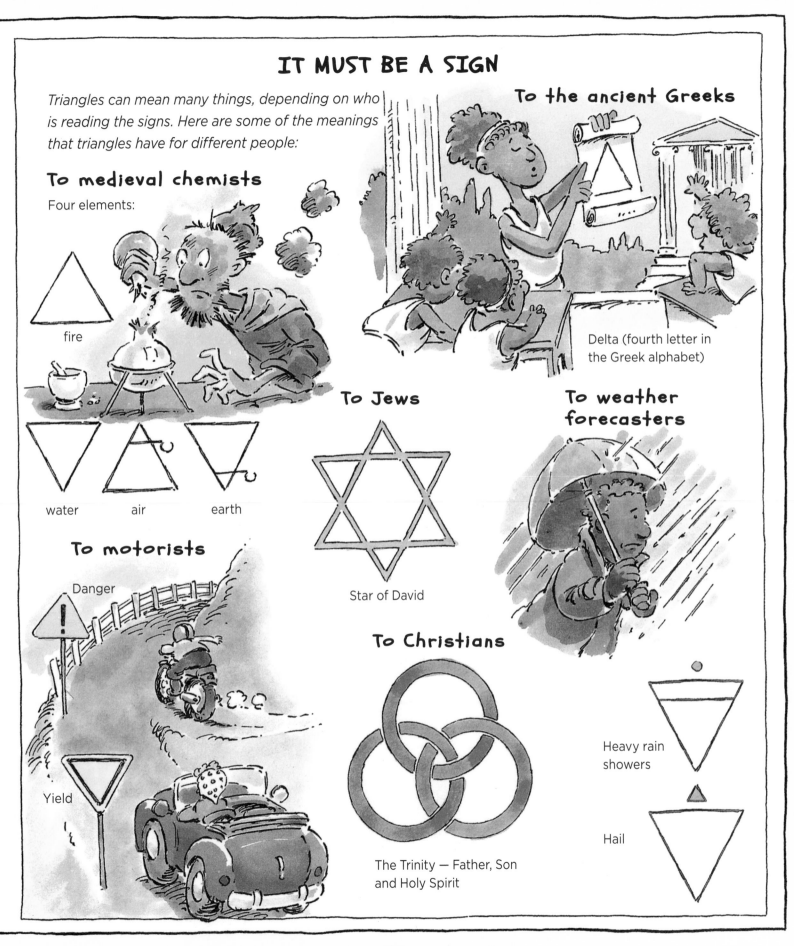

To medieval chemists

Four elements:

fire

water   air   earth

To the ancient Greeks

Delta (fourth letter in the Greek alphabet)

To Jews

Star of David

To weather forecasters

Heavy rain showers

Hail

To motorists

Danger

Yield

To Christians

The Trinity — Father, Son and Holy Spirit

NEWTON'S PRISM

Have you ever wondered about the mini-rainbow that you see when light shines through an aquarium or a piece of glass? Why does this happen? The great scientist Isaac Newton wondered about this, too, and in 1665 he began experimenting with light, lenses and prisms. He was intrigued by the fact that when sunlight passes through a glass prism, the light comes out in separate colored bands. In one experiment, he arranged the shutters on his window to allow only a narrow beam of sunlight into the room. Then he held a prism in this light beam. He saw that the light passing through the prism fell onto the far wall in the colors of the rainbow — red, orange, yellow, green, blue, indigo and violet.

With more experimenting, he discovered that light traveling through a prism fans out into separate bands of color because the prism bends some of the light more than it bends others. Red light travels fastest and is bent the least in passing through the prism. Violet light travels slowest and is bent the most. That's why the red band is always on the top and the violet band is always on the bottom of a rainbow, with the other colors ranged in between. During a shower, falling water droplets act like little prisms to split light into its colors to make a rainbow. If you want to try Newton's experiment, you can buy a prism in a science store, or you can make your own light-catcher by growing an alum crystal.

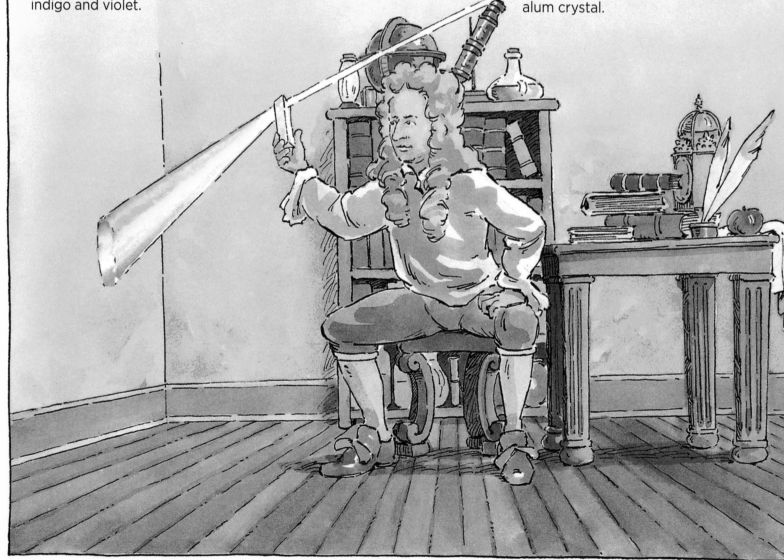

Grow an alum crystal

An alum crystal has the shape of an octahedron. Hang your crystal in a window, and its eight triangular faces will catch the sun to make mini-rainbows.

You'll need:

- water
- a measuring cup
- alum (short for aluminum potassium sulfate; found in drugstores or in the spice section of grocery stores)
- measuring spoon
- a bowl
- white thread
- a paper coffee filter (or several layers of paper towel)
- a glass jar
- a pencil
- cardboard

1. Have an adult pour 60 mL (¼ c.) of boiling water into the measuring cup.

2. Add 30 mL (2 tbsp.) alum to the water and stir to dissolve. There will be a few grains of alum at the bottom of the cup that won't dissolve.

3. Pour the alum solution into the bowl and set it aside for a few days on a shelf where it won't be disturbed.

4. When crystals have formed in the bottom of the bowl, pour off the alum solution. Examine the crystals. Pick out the one that is biggest and best formed to use as a seed crystal. A well-shaped crystal will have triangular faces.

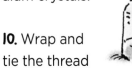

5. Cut a length of white thread as long as your forearm. Tie one end around the seed crystal and set the crystal aside until you have finished steps 6 to 8.

6. Put 60 mL (4 tbsp.) of alum into a measuring cup.

7. Have an adult add small amounts of boiling water gradually to the cup containing the alum. (You need boiling water because more alum dissolves in hot water than in water at room temperature.) Between each new addition of water, stir well to dissolve the alum. Keep adding water gradually until almost all the alum has dissolved.

8. Let the solution cool. (If you put your seed crystal into a hot solution, the crystal might dissolve instead of grow.)

9. Pour the cooled solution through the coffee filter into the glass jar to strain out any remaining undissolved alum crystals.

10. Wrap and tie the thread around a pencil as shown. Use the pencil to hang the crystal in the alum solution in the glass jar. The crystal should be in the middle of the solution, not too close to the walls of the jar.

11. Cover the jar with a piece of cardboard and set it on a shelf for two weeks or more. Watch the crystal grow.

S. TETRAHEDRON

Can you use only six toothpicks to make four equilateral triangles? Give up? No matter how many ways you arrange the toothpicks on a flat table, you can't solve this puzzle in two dimensions. But if you work in three dimensions, the problem is easy. Here's how. With three toothpicks, form a flat triangle on the table, using little balls of modeling clay to hold the corners together. Use the other three toothpicks to make a fourth vertex in the air as shown. With your six toothpicks, you have made four equilateral triangles. The four triangles are the sides, or faces, of a tetrahedron.

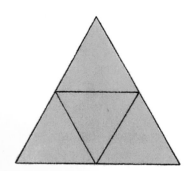

This net can be used for constructing a tetrahedron. You can make a larger net by tracing around a cardboard equilateral triangle four times to produce this arrangement of four triangles. Then cut out and fold along the lines.

Another way to visualize a tetrahedron is to stack four oranges together. If you could draw lines joining the centers of the four oranges, you would have a tetrahedron.

As you might guess, the tetrahedron is a very strong and stable shape. This is because each of its triangular sides is so strong. The tetrahedron is the polyhedron (many-sided solid shape) with the fewest possible sides. It also has the least possible volume, or space inside it, in relation to its outside surface. This large surface area makes the tetrahedron a good shape for a space satellite. One of the world's tiniest satellites is a tetrahedron with sides of 13 cm (5 in.). No matter how it tumbles around in space it will always have one or more sides toward the sun to absorb energy and one or more sides away from the sun for cooling.

Make a tetrahedral gift box

Here's a great way to put tetrahedron to work — make a tetrahedral gift box.

You'll need:
- paper (any size and color, even a big piece of newspaper)
- a pencil
- a compass
- scissors
- sticky tape

1. Draw the largest circle your compass will make — this will make a gift box large enough to hold something the size of a golf ball. Mark the center of the circle with a dot. Cut out the circle. (If you want a gift box big enough to hold something the size of a grapefruit, use a dinner plate to draw the circle. Cut out the circle and fold it in half twice to find the circle's center at the intersection of the two fold lines.)

2. To get the first side of a triangle, fold any point on the outside, or circumference, of the circle so that the point touches the center of the circle where you put the dot.

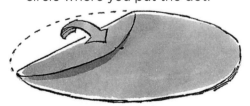

3. Make a second fold as shown, so that the second fold starts at one end of the first fold line and the circumference touches the dot.

4. Make the third side of the triangle by folding the remaining circumference to touch the dot. (If your triangle doesn't have three sharp, well-formed angles, you should unfold it and start again.)

5. Fold one of the sides in half to find its midpoint. Fold the opposite vertex down to touch this midpoint. Sharpen the fold line by running your thumbnail over it. You now have a small triangle in between two others.

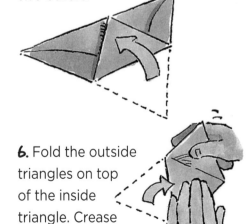

6. Fold the outside triangles on top of the inside triangle. Crease the fold lines.

7. To form a tetrahedron, join the vertices of the original large triangle as shown. Put your present inside, tape the sides shut and add a celebration bow, if you like.

As a gift-box variation for a flat present, make a cut-off, or truncated, tetrahedron. There are just a few more steps.

8. Skip step 7. After step 6, unfold to get the original large triangle. Fold the vertices in to touch the dot at the center of the circle. Crease the fold lines. You now have a hexagon.

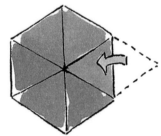

9. Fold the sides up and interlock to make this flattened shape. Put your present inside, and tape your box shut.

Tetrahedral puzzlers

These two brainteasers are sometimes sold in gift shops, but you can make them yourself, following these instructions.

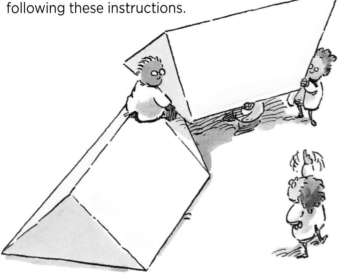

Tetrahedron match-up

It's harder than you might think to match up these two identical puzzle pieces to form a tetrahedron.

You'll need:

- Bristol board
- a ruler
- a pencil
- a compass
- scissors
- sticky tape

1. Construct an equilateral triangle with sides of 15 cm (5 in.) — see "Dissection puzzle" on page 90 for instructions on how to draw an equilateral triangle using a compass.

2. Measure the sides with your ruler, and mark the points that divide the sides into thirds — each segment will be 5 cm (2 in.). Make your measurements as exact as possible, so that the edges of the puzzle piece will fit together neatly later.

3. Construct a square on the middle segment of one side. (Squares have sides that are all the same length and right angles of 90°.)

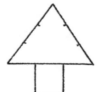

4. Draw four lines as shown to join the division points you have marked on the sides of the equilateral triangle.

5. Use the ruler and the point of the compass to score the lines inside the shape. Scoring the lines makes the cardboard easier to fold.

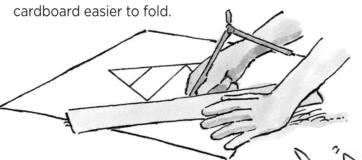

6. Cut out the shape you have drawn, which should look a bit like an Evergreen tree. Cut off the small triangle on the top.

7. Fold along the scored lines. Tape the sides together to finish the puzzle piece.

8. Make a second puzzle piece, exactly the same as the first one.

Now comes the tricky part. Can you fit these pieces together to make a tetrahedron? Give up? (See page 181 for the answer.)

Grape puzzle

The challenge in this puzzle is to stack 20 spheres so that they form a tetrahedron.

You'll need:

- 20 seedless grapes, all the same size (you could use modeling clay balls instead)
- 6 wooden toothpicks

1. Put four grapes on a toothpick as shown. Break off the extra length of the toothpick.

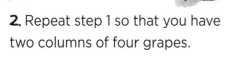

2. Repeat step 1 so that you have two columns of four grapes.

3. Put three grapes on a toothpick. Break off the extra length of toothpick.

4. Repeat step 3 three more times so that you have four columns of three grapes.

5. Arrange these six columns to make a tetrahedron. (See page 181 for the answer.)

Here's a hint. Each face of the tetrahedron will look like this.

BUCKY BUILDING

When the great American architect Buckminster Fuller was in kindergarten in 1899, his teacher asked the class to try using toothpicks and peas to make houses. Everyone made cubes — everyone except for Bucky. He fitted his peas and toothpicks together into triangles. Then he combined his triangles into tetrahedra and octahedra, which he could put together to fill up space without leaving any gaps. His teacher was so amazed by his space-filling triangles that she called in another teacher to admire them.

Why didn't Bucky make rectangular houses, just like everyone else? It turned out that he was almost blind, and had never clearly seen the rectangular world around him, where walls and ceilings meet at right angles. So he used his sense of touch, discovering for himself how triangles hold their shape and make solid structures. Fifty years later, he became world famous for designs based on what he called the octet truss — the same shape he had discovered in his kindergarten classroom.

Unlike cubes, tetrahedra won't pack together to fill space without leaving gaps in between. Packing tetrahedra is more like packing marbles, where air holes are left in between. But if you use octahedra and tetrahedra together, you can completely fill space. Buckminster Fuller called this shape, combining octahedra and tetrahedra, an octet truss.

Toothpick architecture

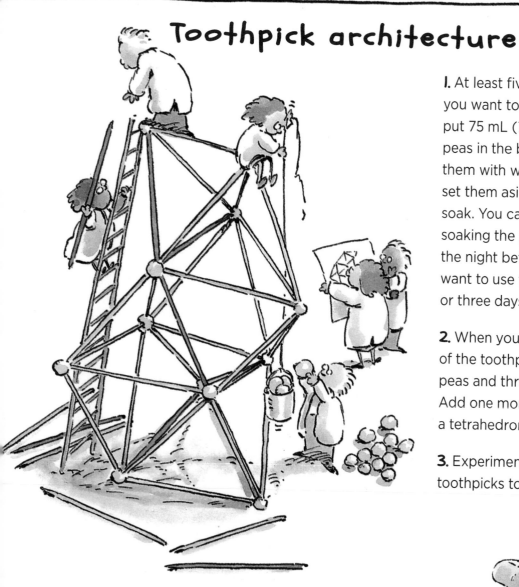

I. At least five hours before you want to start building, put 75 mL (⅓ c.) of dried peas in the bowl, cover them with water and set them aside to soak. You can start soaking the peas the night before you want to use them. But don't leave them soaking for two or three days, or they will start to sprout.

2. When you are ready to start building, poke the ends of the toothpicks into the peas as shown. With three peas and three toothpicks, you can make a triangle. Add one more pea and three more sticks and you have a tetrahedron.

3. Experiment with different ways to connect toothpicks to make towers and buildings.

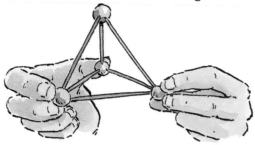

4. Put your creations on a shelf to dry. After a day or two, the peas will dry out and shrink and will hold the toothpicks securely.

Check out for yourself Buckminster Fuller's theories on building with triangles. Make your own toothpick architecture, and compare the shape-holding power of triangles and squares.

You'll need:
- a bowl
- water
- some dried peas (whole peas, not split peas)
- a box of round, cocktail toothpicks. The toothpicks should be pointed on each end. (Use colored toothpicks to make your creations more fun.)

ALEXANDER GRAHAM BELL AND THE TETRAHEDRON

Long before Buckminster Fuller was singing the praises of the tetrahedron, Alexander Graham Bell, the inventor of the telephone, was building them — hundreds of them. He made windbreaks, kites and cabins from tetrahedra. You might think a tetrahedron would be a good shape for a cabin because there would be so few walls to build — only four. Alexander Graham Bell and his wife seemed to find their cabin comfortable, but most people would find it too cramped inside. The tetrahedron has the least possible inside space in relation to its outside surface.

After Bell invented the telephone, he devoted

his time to inventing a flying machine. His dream was to build a kite that would carry a person into the air. Starting with a tetrahedrally shaped kite as a building block, he joined many small kites together to make giant ones. During his experiments, he made about 1200 tetrahedral kites. The biggest one, called the Cygnet, was made from 3393 tetrahedrally shaped cells. In 1907, this kite hoisted a man 50 m (165 ft.) into the air. Some of Bell's experimental kites are in the Bell Museum on Cape Breton Island in Nova Scotia, Canada. This museum was built featuring — guess what shape — the triangle, of course!

6. PYRAMIDS

The sides of a pyramid all meet at one point called the vertex. This means that its top half is much smaller and lighter than its bottom half. When a pyramid is sitting on its base, it's like this bottle of salad dressing — very stable because most of its weight is below the midpoint. (Of course, if you stand the bottle on its top, the slightest shake will make it topple over.)

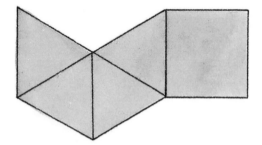

This net for making a pyramid uses a square base and four equilateral triangles.

So what's a pyramid called when its base is a triangle? You guessed it — a tetrahedron. Take another look at the tetrahedral gift box you made on page 111.

The pyramid's stability explains why it's used for monuments that are intended to last forever. The ancient Egyptians built pyramids of stone for their Pharaohs' tombs, which were to house their souls throughout eternity. When Americans wanted a symbol of stability and eternity for their one-dollar bill, they chose the stone pyramid.

These pyramids all have square bases. But pyramids can also have bases that are triangles, pentagons, hexagons and so on. They are still pyramids as long as they have sides that are triangles meeting at one point. How many faces will a pyramid have? That's easy — the same number of faces as the number of sides in its base.

LEONARDO'S PARACHUTE

Pyramids don't all have to be as heavy as stone. In 1485, Leonardo da Vinci, the great Italian sculptor, painter and inventor, designed this lightweight pyramid as a parachute.

Make a pyramid

Experiment with pyramids of different bases.

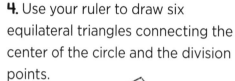
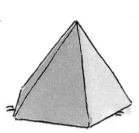
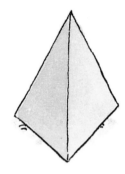

You'll need:

- Bristol board or cardboard
- a compass
- a pencil
- a ruler
- scissors
- glue

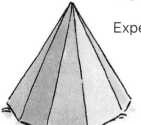

1. Use your compass to draw a circle on the Bristol board.

2. Keep the same compass opening that you used for the circle. Mark a point anywhere on the outside of the circle. Put the compass foot on this point and draw an arc to intersect the circle at a second point.

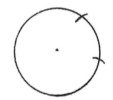

3. Continue around the circle in the same way, using your compass to draw four more division points. You have now divided the circle into six equal parts.

4. Use your ruler to draw six equilateral triangles connecting the center of the circle and the division points.

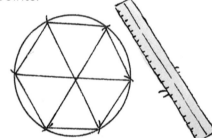

5. Cut out the hexagon.

6. Cut along one of the lines that connects a division point to the center.

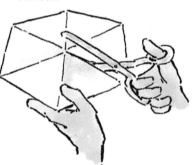

7. Using the pointed foot of the compass, score the other five lines. Fold along the lines.

8. Experiment with pyramids with different-shaped bases. Overlap one of the triangular faces to make a five-sided pyramid. Overlap three faces to get a tetrahedron. Finally, overlap two faces to make a square-based pyramid. Glue the two overlapping faces together.

Volume of a square pyramid

Turn the square-based pyramid upside-down. If you filled this hollow container with water, how many containersful would it take to fill up a square prism with the same base and height? (See page 181 for the answer.)

THE EGYPTIAN PYRAMIDS

The Great Pyramid is one of the Seven Wonders of the World, as silent and mysterious today as when it was first built 4500 years ago. It's the largest of three pyramids at Giza on the river Nile. It was made from more than 2 million stone blocks weighing 2.3 metric tons each, and it covers an area the size of ten city blocks. Why build such a gigantic monument? The Great Pyramid was a royal tomb for the Pharaoh Khufu. But some Egyptologists think it may also have been a gigantic public works program to give jobs to Egyptian farmers while the Nile was flooding their lands each fall. Others think it served as a temple for the sun god Re. It does seem to have been built as a gigantic astrological instrument for watching the sun and stars and for establishing true north. It can't be just a coincidence that the four corners of the pyramid's square base are like a compass pointing exactly to the north, south, east and west.

At the center of the Great Pyramid were the Pharaoh's burial chambers. These chambers could be reached by a steeply climbing corridor 47 m (153 ft.) long. After Khufu's funeral, huge granite blocks were slid down this passageway to close off the burial chambers and protect the golden treasures buried with him. But even Egyptian engineering genius couldn't keep out robbers, who broke into the burial chamber and stole the treasures inside.

AZTEC PYRAMIDS

The Indians of Central and South America also built colossal pyramids. The Pyramid of the Sun, near present-day Mexico City, once formed the center of a great civilization that flourished about 1500 years ago. This pyramid has two giant staircases on the north and south walls that lead to a sanctuary on the top.

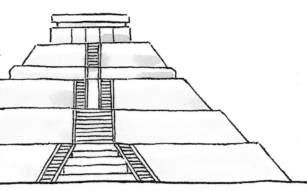

CIRCLES

What pattern do you see when you throw a stone into a still pond or look at the sawed-off stump of a tree? Circles. Look around — you likely see lots of circles. Circles are flat, with only two dimensions — length and width. But add a little thickness and you have a disk like a coin. Spin a coin around on its edge and you get a three-dimensional sphere with length, width and depth. The orange you eat for breakfast is a sphere, and so are the planets, soap bubbles and a drop of water. Take a circle, stretch it up into a column, and you have a cylinder. Tin cans are cylinders, and so are the trunks of trees and the bones in your legs.

You can make circles with your body — hugs are circles. Whirl around fast in one spot, and you are spinning in circles. Join hands with your friends, and you can do a circle dance.

When you read the Circles section, you will blow some super-bubbles; read about the most famous stone circle of all, Stonehenge; experiment to find out which shapes are strongest for constructing buildings; learn about things that spin, roll or twirl; find out why castles have round towers; bake some yummy circles; and much more.

1. AMAZING CIRCLES

If you fold a circle in half anywhere, the two halves always exactly match. Try spinning a circle around like a wheel of fortune. It takes the same space as if it were standing still. If you roll a circle along the ground, it's always the same height. So circles make good wheels. Imagine riding a bicycle with square or rectangular tires. Ouch! Circles are special because each point on a circle is exactly the same distance from the center. This means that circles are perfectly symmetrical.

GIOTTO'S O

Pope Benedict XI wanted to find the best painter in Italy to decorate the first St. Peter's Cathedral in Rome. So he sent a messenger to visit the great masters and get samples of their drawings. Finally, the messenger arrived at Giotto's workshop in Florence, where the painter was hard at work. When Giotto heard what the Pope wanted, he got out a fresh piece of paper and dipped his brush in red paint. Holding his arm close to his body, he made a perfect circle. "Here is your drawing," he said. The messenger thought Giotto was kidding and asked, "Won't you send anything else?" "Even this is too much," said Giotto. "Give it to the Pope

along with all the other artists' drawings, and it will be appreciated." So the messenger gave the circle drawing to the Pope, explaining how it had been drawn freehand and without a compass. The Pope and his art advisers recognized immediately Giotto's outstanding talent for drawing. And that's how Giotto came to Rome to paint for the Pope.

Drawing circles

Unless you are a Giotto, you might not be able to draw freehand a perfectly symmetrical circle, but here's how to draw one with some simple equipment.

You'll need:

- a compass
- paper
- a pencil
- string
- a pin

I. To draw a circle exactly the size you want, use a compass. Put the pointed end or foot of the compass on the paper just where you want the center of the circle to be. Rotate the other end around it to draw your circle. Make sure the compass opening doesn't change in the middle of drawing your circle. (If it does change, the line you are drawing won't end up at its starting point and you won't have a circle.)

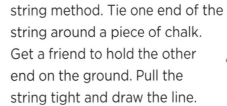

2. To make bigger or smaller circles, change the distance between the two compass feet. The circle you draw will always be twice as wide as the distance between the two compass feet — this distance is the circle's radius.

3. To draw bigger circles than your compass will allow, you can use a pencil and string. Tie one end of the string around the pencil. Use a pin to hold the other end of the string to the center of your paper. Pull the string tight and draw a line around the pin until you get back to your starting point. To draw a really big circle on pavement, you can use this same string method. Tie one end of the string around a piece of chalk. Get a friend to hold the other end on the ground. Pull the string tight and draw the line.

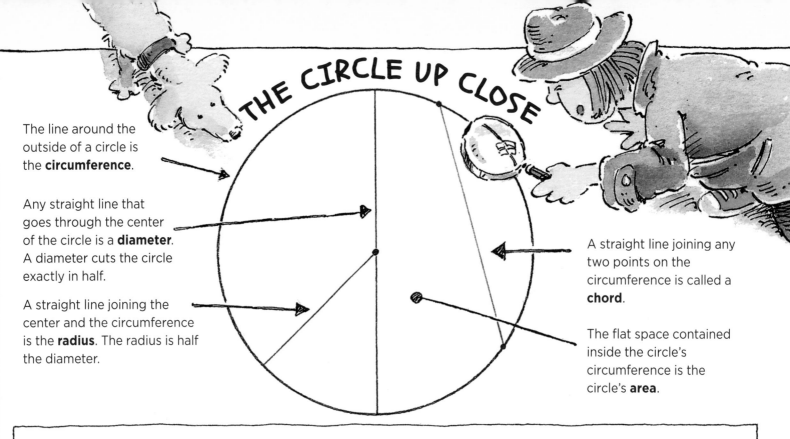

The line around the outside of a circle is the **circumference**.

Any straight line that goes through the center of the circle is a **diameter**. A diameter cuts the circle exactly in half.

A straight line joining the center and the circumference is the **radius**. The radius is half the diameter.

A straight line joining any two points on the circumference is called a **chord**.

The flat space contained inside the circle's circumference is the circle's **area**.

CIRCLE FACTS

1. *After you've drawn a circle by tracing around the outside of a round object such as a can or plate, how can you find its center? Cut out the circle with scissors. Fold it in half in two different places. The point where the two folds, or diameters, cross is the exact center of the circle.*

Once you have found the center, it's easy to figure out the radius. The radius is the distance between your compass points when one point is on the center and the other point is anywhere on the circumference.

2. *You can draw a right-angled triangle by joining the diameter of a circle to a third point anywhere on the circumference of a circle.*

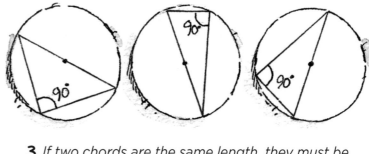

3. *If two chords are the same length, they must be the same distance from the center of a circle.*

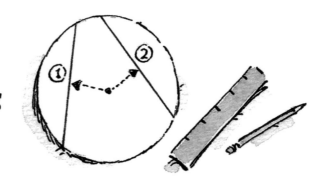

Fold some circles

What can you do with circles you have drawn? Try folding them to make some other great shapes — triangles, squares, hexagons, even stars.

1. Use a compass to draw a circle on your paper. Don't make your circle too small — set your compass points about 10 cm (4 in.) apart. This distance will be the radius of your circle. Cut out the circle.

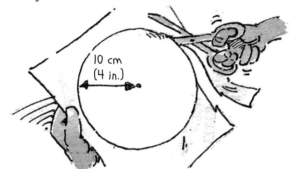

2. Fold the circle in half. Fold it in half again parallel to, or alongside, the first fold. Open the circle out and you will see three parallel fold lines.

3. Now fold the circle in half again so that your new fold line intersects, or cuts across, the other folds at right angles as shown. Fold it in half again as before.

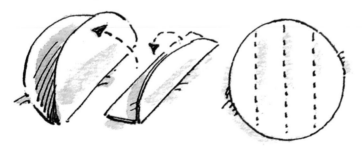

4. Open the circle. You now have six fold lines that touch the circumference in 12 places called division points.

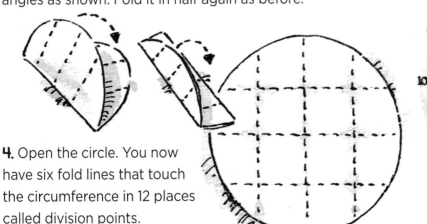

5. Use your ruler to draw lines to connect these 12 division points. Connect every point and you get a 12-sided polygon. Mathematicians call this 12-sided shape a dodecagon.

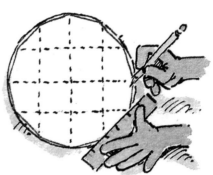

6. Try some variations. Connect every second point to get a hexagon (six sides). Connect every third point (skip two) and you get a square. Connect every fourth point (skip three) to get a triangle.

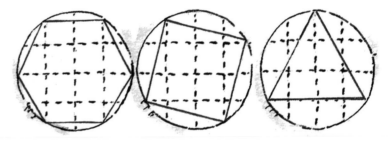

7. If you want to get fancy, make this star pattern. Pick a division point and look for a second point exactly opposite it along the diameter. Connect your first point with the two division points on either side of the second point. For example, connect point 12 with points 5 and 7. Repeat for each division point.

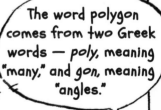

The word polygon comes from two Greek words — *poly*, meaning "many," and *gon*, meaning "angles."

Measuring circles

Suppose you had something circular like a plate and you wanted to know how big it was. How could you measure it? If you knew the circle's radius (see page 126), it would be easy to double the radius to get the diameter. This way you'd know how big the circle is across the middle. But you might also want to know how big the circle is around the outside — its circumference. Or how much space there is inside the circle — its area.

Look at these two plates. It's easy to see that the plate with the bigger diameter also has a bigger circumference with more area inside it. But how much more? And how can you measure it? With an amazing number called pi (named for the Greek letter π and pronounced "pie"). Thousands of years ago, mathematicians made the discovery that no matter how big a circle is, the number you get by dividing its circumference by its diameter is always the same. This number is called pi.

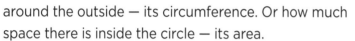

Here's how you can figure out the approximate value of pi.

You'll need:

• a piece of string
• a cylinder (such as a can)
• scissors
• a pencil
• paper

I. Wrap a piece of string tightly around the cylinder. Cut the string so that it is exactly long enough to go around the cylinder. (This string will be the length of the circumference of the cylinder.)

2. Trace the outline of the bottom of the cylinder on a piece of paper and cut out the circle.

3. Fold the circle in half to make a diameter.

4. Hold the string taut, match the diameter against the string and note the end point. Starting at this end point, match the diameter against the string as before. Repeat until you run out of string. How many diameters could you fit along the length of string?

What's happening?

You probably made the diameter fit three times along the string and then had a bit of string left over. So the circumference divided by the diameter, or pi, is a bit more than three. The ancient Greeks worked out the value of pi to four decimal places — 3.1416.

As long as you know the value of pi, there's only one more thing you really need to know to measure a circle — its radius. Knowing pi and the circle's radius, you can always figure out its circumference and its area.

The circumference is two times pi (π) multiplied by the radius (r). That's $2 \times \pi \times r$ or $2\pi r$.

The area of a circle (the amount of space contained inside the circle) is pi times the radius multiplied by itself. That's $\pi \times r \times r$ or πr^2.

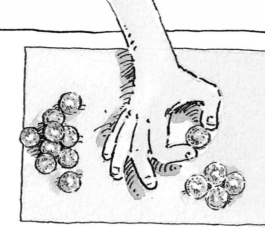

SPACE TEST

Put a dime on the table. How many other dimes can you fit around the first dime, touching it? Do you get the same answer if you try this space test using nickels? How about quarters?

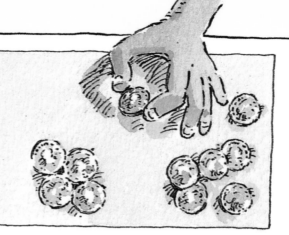

EASY AS PI

Gravestone π

Working out pi more accurately than 3.1416 is time-consuming and not very useful. (Ten decimals are enough to calculate the circumference of a sphere the size of the Earth.) But some mathematicians can't turn down a challenge. Leudolph van Ceulen, a Dutch mathematician, spent much of his life calculating pi to 35 decimal places. When he died in 1610, the numbers 2 8 8 were carved on his tombstone — the 33rd, 34th and 35th decimal places of pi.

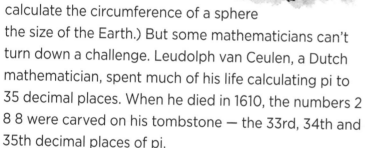

A π record

π = 3.1415926535897932384626433832795028841 7169399375105820974944592307816406286208 998628034825 and so on forever. So what is now the most accurate measurement of pi? With the help of computers, the value of pi has been calculated to trillions of digits. The world record for calculating the value of pi never lasts very long because there is no final answer — the decimal places go on forever.

Sci fi π

On an episode of *Star Trek*, Spock used pi to outwit a smart but nasty computer. This out-of-control computer had decided to destroy the Starship Enterprise. Spock tricked the computer by asking it to figure out the value of pi. Since this calculation goes on forever, it kept the evil computer very busy. Meanwhile, the crew had time to discover how to shut down the computer.

π memory test

How many numbers in the value of pi can you remember? Most people can get to 3.14 or possibly 3.1416. Since the value of pi is a string of numbers that goes on forever with no pattern, it's impossible to memorize. But in 2005, a Chinese man recited from memory the value of pi to 67 890 places. According to *The Guinness Book of Records*, it took him 24 hours and 4 minutes.

CIRCLE IMPOSSIBILITIES

Then, in 1989, Miklós Laczkovich of Hungary discovered a new way of squaring the circle — by cutting up the circle into tiny pieces and rearranging them into a square. He figured that to make a square with no gaps and no overlapping pieces it would take 10^{50} pieces. That's 10 multiplied by itself 50 times.

Mathematicians like challenges and don't give up easily. Calculating the final value of pi isn't their only impossible circle challenge. There's also "squaring the circle." People have been trying for 4000 years to make a square that encloses an area exactly equal to the area of a given circle, using only a ruler and a compass. By 1775, there were so many attempted formulas that the French Academy declared it wouldn't examine any more solutions to this puzzle. No one has ever succeeded in squaring the circle with a ruler and compass, and no one ever will. In 1882, a German mathematician proved the task was impossible.

Why do elephants have round feet?

To step on the lily pads.

Why is an aspirin small, white and circular?

Because if it were big, gray and wrinkly, it would be an elephant.

Make a Moebius strip

Here's a neat circle trick that turns an ordinary strip of paper into an incredible loop.

You'll need:

• a strip of paper about 30 cm (12 in.) long and 2.5 cm (1 in.) wide
• tape
• a colored marker
• scissors

I. Take a strip of paper and bring the ends together. Give one end a half-turn and tape the ends together. You've made a Moebius strip.

2. Draw a line along the paper band down its middle. Start anywhere and keep going, without lifting your marker, until you get back to your starting place. Surprised? Which side is "inside" and which is "outside"? Your line goes along both sides and yet you did not cross an edge. This means your loop has only one side. An ant would be able to walk on it from any spot to any other spot without ever crossing an edge.

3. Try something else. Cut along the line you drew. If you cut an ordinary loop of paper through the middle, it separates into two narrower loops. How many sides does the cut-in-half Moebius strip have? (To find out, draw a line as before along the length of the band till you get back to your starting place.) How many twists does it have now?

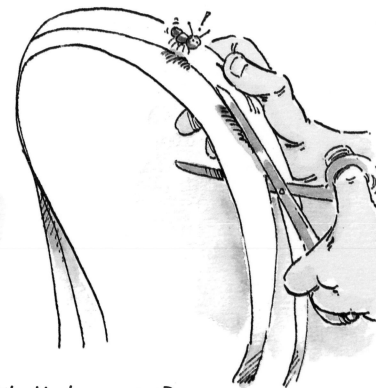

What's happening?

The Moebius strip has only one surface and one edge. The German mathematician August Ferdinand Moebius wrote about it in 1858 as an amusing game, but the Moebius strip has turned out to have practical uses. Engineers use them as conveyor belts on assembly lines. An ordinary belt, with an inside and an outside, wears out faster on one side than the other. A Moebius strip, with only one side, wears evenly and lasts longer.

2. LIVING IN CIRCLES

Imagine what it would be like to be completely circle shaped. Instead of having a head and arms and feet and walking upright, you would just roll over and over. That's what the first life forms did. Small ball-shaped creatures, like this radiolarian, lived in the sea, rolling and tossing in the current, with no upside down and no right way up. Just like circles, they had what's called radial symmetry — they looked exactly the same from every direction.

Then life branched off along two different paths. Some life forms became plants, which also have radial symmetry, and some became animals. Take a look at your own body — does it have radial symmetry? Of course not. You definitely have a right-side up, and your left eye is matched by a right eye; your left arm and leg are matched by a right arm and leg. Your left side is the mirror image of your right side, so your body has bilateral symmetry.

Check out these two different kinds of symmetry for yourself. Fold a piece of paper in half and cut out a half circle and doll as shown. When you unfold these shapes, you should have a full circle and paper doll.

Now fold the circle in half along different fold lines. You can fold it in half anywhere, and the two halves will always match up. That's radial symmetry — symmetry in all directions. Now fold the doll in half down the center. The two halves will match — that center fold line is called the axis of symmetry.

What happens if you fold the doll in half any other way? It won't match up. Like your body, the doll has bilateral symmetry with only one axis of symmetry. When you folded your circle, you discovered that it has more than one axis of symmetry.

So why do plants have radial symmetry, while animals have bilateral symmetry? It's because plants stay in one place, and animals move around. Since plants stay rooted, they don't need a front and a back, a right side and a left side. Instead, nearly identical parts grow out from the center in all directions, like the branches on a pine tree. So trees and bushes usually are circular. But since animals move, most have evolved into shapes with bilateral symmetry. A moving animal needs special features on the front of its body. You may have heard jokes about teachers with eyes in the back of their heads. But of course eyes, ears and nose all point frontward — an animal needs to know where it is going toward, not where it is coming from. Since enemies are just as likely to spring from the left as from the right, an animal needs all the same features on its left side as on its right. So, in your own body, your front is very different from your back, but your left side and your right side are mirror images of each other.

Circle prints

Plants grow in circles, and you can find circle shapes in parts of plants, too, such as in fruits and vegetables. Jazz up your notepaper and wrapping paper with these circle designs.

You'll need:

• a knife
• fruit or vegetables such as oranges, lemons, apples, onions, cucumbers, carrots, radishes
• paintbrushes
• tempera paint (various colors)
• paper (if you want to make wrapping paper, use large pieces of recycled newsprint)

I. To make your circle-shaped stamps, cut an apple or an orange in half. Cut thick cross-sections, or slices, from onions, carrots or cucumbers (if you make them too thin, they're hard to hold when you use them as stamps). You might also want to cut a few carrot slices in half to make semi-circles.

2. Use a brush to apply paint to a circle stamp, or dip the stamp into the paint.

3. Press the stamp onto the paper. Don't move it sideways or the paint will blur.

4. Keep making impressions with the same stamp until you run out of paint. With onion or orange stamps, the texture shows through when the paint runs out, making an interesting design.

5. When the paint on the stamp has been used up, apply more. Experiment with different shapes and designs, different colors and different amounts of paint on the stamp.

CIRCLE SIGNS

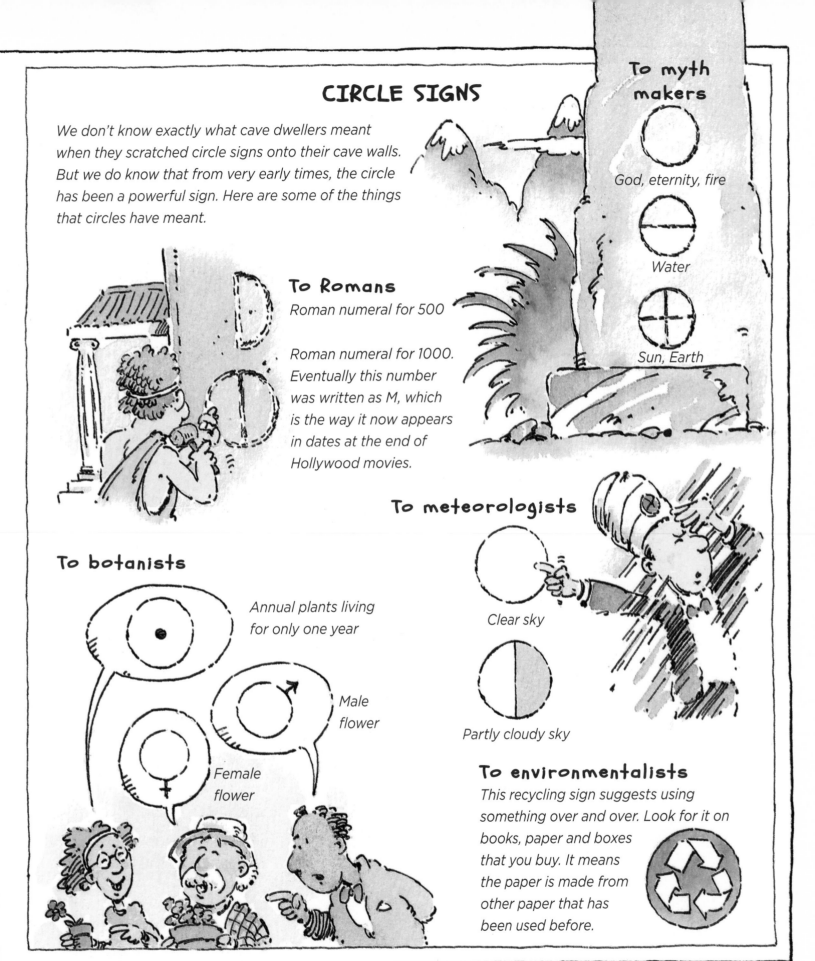

We don't know exactly what cave dwellers meant when they scratched circle signs onto their cave walls. But we do know that from very early times, the circle has been a powerful sign. Here are some of the things that circles have meant.

To myth makers

God, eternity, fire

Water

Sun, Earth

To Romans

Roman numeral for 500

Roman numeral for 1000. Eventually this number was written as M, which is the way it now appears in dates at the end of Hollywood movies.

To botanists

Annual plants living for only one year

Male flower

Female flower

To meteorologists

Clear sky

Partly cloudy sky

To environmentalists

This recycling sign suggests using something over and over. Look for it on books, paper and boxes that you buy. It means the paper is made from other paper that has been used before.

BUILDING IN CIRCLES

Take a piece of string and tie the ends together to form a loop. Put the loop on a table and push it around into different positions — a square, a rectangle, a triangle, a circle. What shape should you make the loop if you want to enclose the largest area possible inside the loop?

Princess Dido knew the answer to this puzzle. According to an ancient Greek legend, her brother Pygmalion murdered her husband. Dido fled with some loyal supporters to the coast of North Africa near modern Tunis. She asked the loyal king to sell her some land so that she could build a new city there. When he said no, she won him over by saying, "Just sell me the amount of land that I can enclose by the hide of an ox." As soon as the king agreed, Dido told her servants to tan an ox hide and cut it up into long, very narrow strips. Then she sewed all the strips together to make one very long leather strip. With this strip, she formed a loop large enough to enclose land for building the new city of Carthage. What shape was Dido's loop? A circle. A loop will contain the most area inside if the loop is in the shape of a circle.

The super circle

Use Queen Dido's cutting trick to amaze your friends. Show them that, with nothing but scissors, you can turn an ordinary index card into a circle big enough to step through.

You'll need:
• an 8 × 13-cm (3 × 5-in.) index card
• scissors

1. Fold the card in half so that the short edges meet.

2. Cut through the folded card as shown. Your first cut should start at the fold. Leave 0.5 cm (¼ in.) uncut.

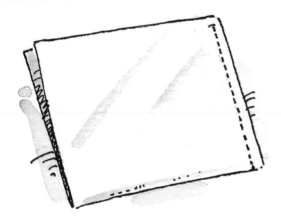

3. Make your second cut alongside the first cut, but this time start your cut on the opposite side of the card. As before, leave 0.5 cm (¼ in.) uncut.

4. Alternate your cuts from side to side until you have made cuts in the whole card as shown. You should end up with an odd number of cuts (13 or 15 cuts, but not 12 or 14). The closer together you make the cuts, the more cuts you'll have and the bigger your super circle will be.

5. Unfold the card and flatten it out. You now have an interesting chain, but to do the magic circle trick you need to make one more cut. Cut through all the folds except for the ones at each end of the card. Voilà! A large loop you can squeeze your whole body through. (If you want to get a cow through your magic circle with lots of room to spare, start with a sheet of exercise paper and make your cuts quite close together.)

3. FAR-OUT CIRCLES

You may not feel that you're moving, but you're actually whirling around the Sun at an average rate of almost 30 km (19 mi.) a second. Our Sun is also hurtling through our star system, the Milky Way, at about 19 km (12 mi.) per second, along with 100 billion other suns that we call stars. The Milky Way goes in circles, too, making one turn every 200 million years. So the universe is one grand circle dance of whirling, twirling, circling and spinning.

It took many centuries of star-gazing to figure out this dance. The ancient Greek astronomer Ptolemy in the second century AD thought that the Earth was right at the center of everything in the universe. It's natural to want to be in the most important place. If you had your choice, where would you rather be? Off somewhere on the edge or right at the center of things? Ptolemy knew where he preferred to be. He claimed that the Earth stood still and that everything else circled around it. People believed him for more than 1500 years.

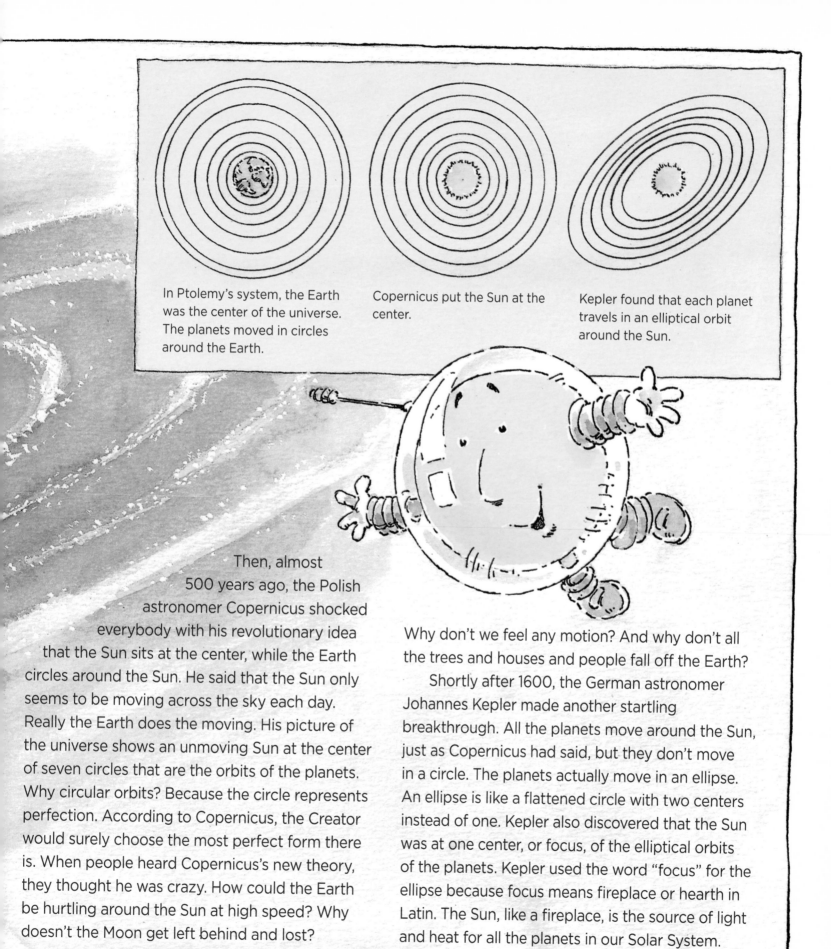

In Ptolemy's system, the Earth was the center of the universe. The planets moved in circles around the Earth.

Copernicus put the Sun at the center.

Kepler found that each planet travels in an elliptical orbit around the Sun.

Then, almost 500 years ago, the Polish astronomer Copernicus shocked everybody with his revolutionary idea that the Sun sits at the center, while the Earth circles around the Sun. He said that the Sun only seems to be moving across the sky each day. Really the Earth does the moving. His picture of the universe shows an unmoving Sun at the center of seven circles that are the orbits of the planets. Why circular orbits? Because the circle represents perfection. According to Copernicus, the Creator would surely choose the most perfect form there is. When people heard Copernicus's new theory, they thought he was crazy. How could the Earth be hurtling around the Sun at high speed? Why doesn't the Moon get left behind and lost?

Why don't we feel any motion? And why don't all the trees and houses and people fall off the Earth?

Shortly after 1600, the German astronomer Johannes Kepler made another startling breakthrough. All the planets move around the Sun, just as Copernicus had said, but they don't move in a circle. The planets actually move in an ellipse. An ellipse is like a flattened circle with two centers instead of one. Kepler also discovered that the Sun was at one center, or focus, of the elliptical orbits of the planets. Kepler used the word "focus" for the ellipse because focus means fireplace or hearth in Latin. The Sun, like a fireplace, is the source of light and heat for all the planets in our Solar System.

Make an ellipse

An ellipse looks like a circle that's been sat on. It's easy to make. If you draw a circle on a stretchy, rubbery substance, you can turn it into an ellipse by stretching out the circle in one direction. But a better way is to use the string method.

You'll need:

- a piece of string about 25 cm (10 in.) long
- a sheet of paper
- a corkboard
- 2 thumbtacks
- a pencil

I. Tie the string together at the ends to form a loop.

2. Place the paper on the corkboard.

3. Locate the thumbtacks about 4 cm (1½ in.) apart and push them part way into the paper and corkboard.

4. Loop the string around the thumbtacks. Put a pencil inside the string loop and pull tight.

5. Keeping the string pulled tight, draw a curve with your pencil until you come back to your starting point. An ellipse!

6. Experiment. You can make bigger or smaller ellipses by changing the length of the string you use to make the loop. You can also get different results by moving the thumbtacks farther apart or closer together. The thumbtacks are the foci or centers of your ellipse. What happens if you put your thumbtacks really close together?

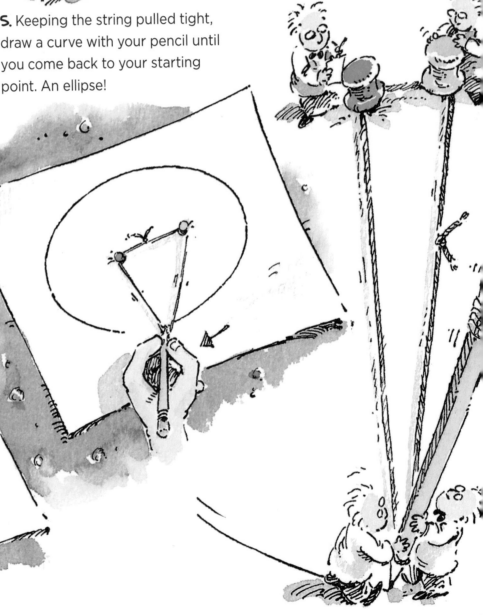

The expanding circle trick

Challenge your friends to the expanding circle mystery.

You'll need:

• a pencil
• a dime
• an index card
• scissors
• a quarter

I. Trace the outline of a dime on the index card.

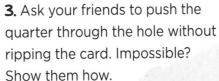

2. Carefully cut out around the outline, making a dime-sized hole in the card.

3. Ask your friends to push the quarter through the hole without ripping the card. Impossible? Show them how.

4. Fold the card along the diameter of the cut-out circle. Put the quarter between the folds in the card so that it sticks out the hole in the card. The hole is too small to let the quarter go through.

5. Bend the fold of the card down as shown. Now the quarter passes through easily.

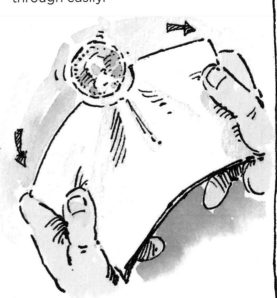

How does it work?

By bending the card, you turn the circle into an ellipse with a bigger diameter — big enough to let the quarter slip through.

STONE CIRCLES

About 900 stone circles are still left in England from prehistoric times, but Stonehenge is the most famous of these mysterious constructions. This circle of huge stones is so mind-boggling that 1 million people visit it every year. How did it get there and why was it built? Some used to say that Stonehenge was made by Egyptian pyramid builders who came to England. Others said it was made by Martians. But many astronomers now think that Stonehenge was built by prehistoric

people as an observatory to watch the sun, identify the longest day of the year and predict eclipses of the moon.

We now know that Stonehenge was actually made in stages over a very long period. Stone-age people began the outer part almost 4500 years ago. First they dug a circular ditch. Inside the ditch, they built a circular wall with an inside diameter of about 97 m (320 ft.) — almost the length of a football field. This wall of earth was about 6 m (20 ft.) thick and as high as a tall person

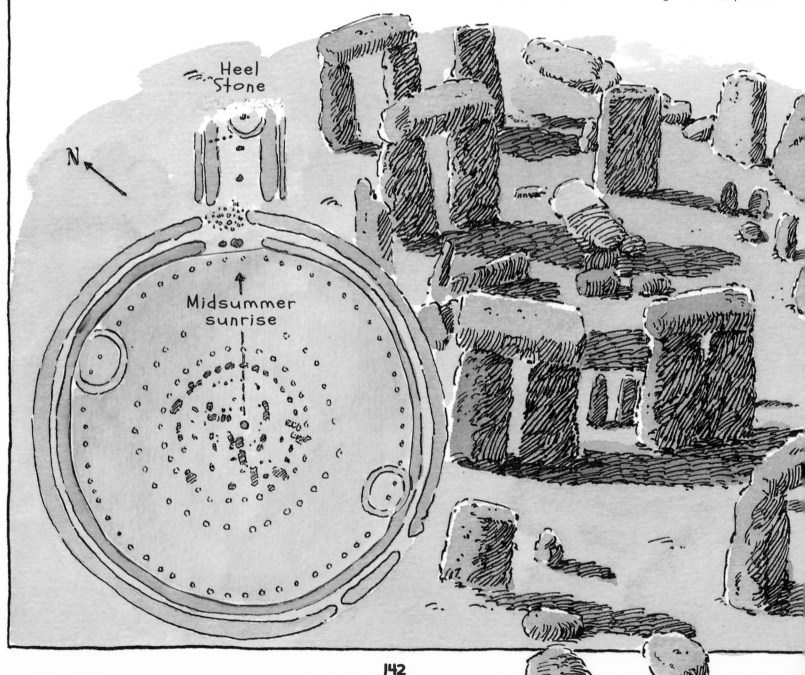

Heel Stone

N

Midsummer sunrise

— that's a lot of earth to move with only deer antler picks and other primitive equipment. Workers left a gap in the wall so that people at the center of the circle could look out and see a huge rock, called the Heel Stone, outside the circle. The line that joins the center of the circle to the Heel Stone points to the rising sun on June 21 — the longest day of the year, when the days begin to get shorter.

The famous inner circle of stones wasn't built for another 1000 years, by different people with a different language. Its huge upright stones, each weighing as much as 12 elephants, had to be dragged 30 km (19 mi.) over hilly country to the Stonehenge site. Cross pieces, or lintels, were fitted on top of the upright stones. Amazingly, five of these lintels are still in place, even after 3500 years. At dawn on the summer solstice on June 21, you can look from the center of the circle through the stone archway to the Heel Stone and see the rising sun.

MYSTERY CIRCLES

Mystery circles have been appearing in farmers' fields. Something has been flattening out crops of wheat and barley to form perfect circles. In 1990, more than 400 circles were counted in southern England alone, some as big as 60 m (197 ft.) in diameter. Crop circles are not new. They were spotted during the Middle Ages by people who thought they were the work of "mowing devils."

Now some people say the circles are doodles drawn by extraterrestrials, while others think the crops are being flattened into circles by whirling winds. However, most insist there has to be a better explanation — they just don't agree on what the explanation is. So far, the most likely theory seems to be that many of the circles are actually pranks that have evolved into an international phenomenon.

Make a sundial

You don't have to build a Stonehenge to track the sun. You can put a stick in the ground in full sunshine and watch how the shadow moves. In the early morning, the shadow is long and points west, away from the sun. At noon, when the sun is overhead, the shadow is short. Toward evening, the shadow lengthens again and points east. So a stick in the ground can give you a rough idea of the time of day. For something more accurate, you can make a sundial to tell you the hour.

You need two essential parts for a sundial: the shadow maker and the dial. The shadow maker is called the *gnomon* (a Greek word meaning one who knows). The shadow falls on a surface with markings on it, called the dial (from the Latin word *dies*, meaning day).

You'll need:

- a ruler
- a pencil
- a square piece of corrugated cardboard 30 × 30 cm (12 × 12 in.)
- a compass
- a protractor
- an oblong piece of corrugated cardboard at least 13 × 30 cm (5 × 12 in.)
- scissors
- masking tape

1. Use your ruler to draw a line connecting the midpoints of two sides of the cardboard square. Use the sharp point of the compass to score along this line (don't press hard enough to tear the cardboard). Fold along the scored line.

2. Draw a line parallel to a third side 2.5 cm (1 in.) in from the edge. Measure to find the midpoint of this line.

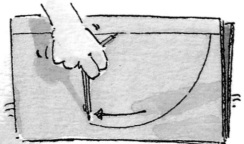

3. Put the compass foot on the midpoint and, below the line, draw a semi-circle with a radius of 10 cm (4 in.).

4. To turn this semi-circle into a dial, you need to divide the semi-circle into 12 equal units. Line up your protractor on the semi-circle as shown, with the center of the protractor on the center of the semi-circle. Read the markings on the outside curve of the protractor, and put a mark on your dial every 15° — where it says 15, 30, 45, 60, 75, 90, etc. — until you have marked off 11 equally spaced points on the outside of the semi-circle.

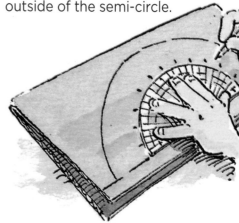

5. Number the points on your dial as shown, going clockwise in this order: 6, 7, 8, 9, 10, 11, 12, 1, 2, 3, 4, 5, 6. (If you live in Australia or elsewhere below the equator, go counter-clockwise.)

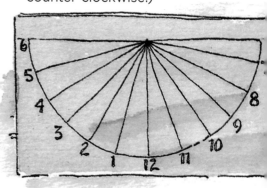

6. Use the sharp foot of the compass to poke a hole through the cardboard at the center of the semi-circle. Push a pencil through the hole. This pencil is your gnomon, or shadow maker. When you get your sundial finished, the gnomon will end up being held at an angle equal to the latitude where you live.

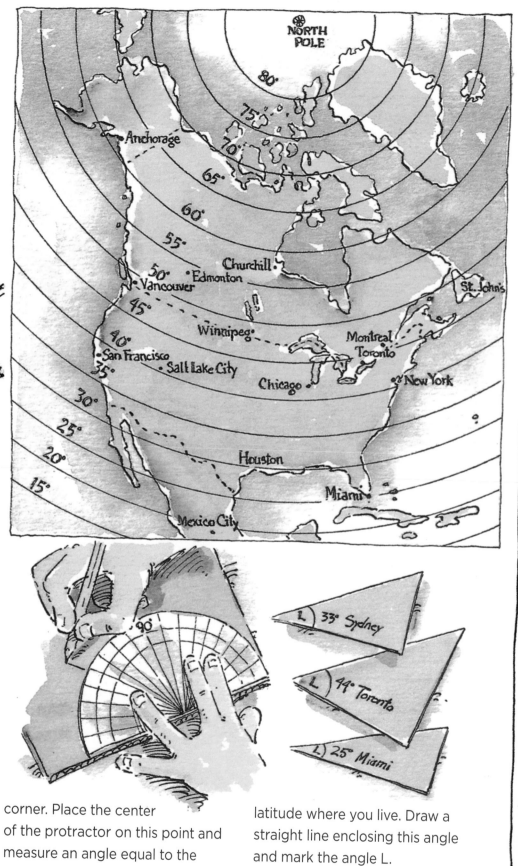

7. Now you'll need to cut out two equal-sized triangular pieces as side supports. The trick is that the size of the triangle you cut depends on the latitude where you live. (One angle of the triangle is 90°, or a right angle. But a second angle should be the degree of latitude where you live. For example, if you live in Toronto, Ontario, your angle should be 44°; if you live in Miami, Florida, it should be 25°; and if you live in Sydney, Australia, it should be 33°. Check the map provided to find your latitude, or look in an atlas.) To make one triangular piece, mark a point on the short side of the cardboard rectangle 9 cm (3½ in.) from the corner. Place the center of the protractor on this point and measure an angle equal to the latitude where you live. Draw a straight line enclosing this angle and mark the angle L.

8. Cut out the triangle. Trace this triangle on the leftover piece of cardboard and cut out a second triangle the same as the first. Mark the angle L.

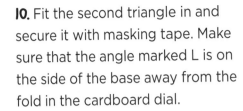

10. Fit the second triangle in and secure it with masking tape. Make sure that the angle marked L is on the side of the base away from the fold in the cardboard dial.

11. Now you are ready to try out your sundial. Pick a spot for your sundial where the sun shines all day. Align the sundial with the tip of the gnomon, or pencil, facing north (south if you live south of the equator). An easy way to line up your sundial correctly the first time is to use your watch — turn the sundial so that the shadow indicates the right time. But if it's

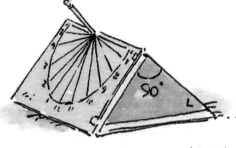

summer, you may have to subtract an hour to adjust for Daylight Savings Time. Check your sundial at different times during the day to see how well it's keeping time.

12. As a final touch, decorate your sundial. You can write a message on it. In 18th-century gardens, sundials carried warnings such as "It's later than you think."

9. In your left hand, hold the cardboard dial folded in half as shown. In your right hand, hold a triangle piece with the 90° angle on top and the angle of latitude (L) on the right as shown. Fit the triangle into the folded cardboard dial. Tape it securely with masking tape.

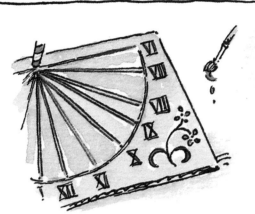

How does it work?

Sundials work because the Earth makes one complete turn every day, going through a full 360° turn in 24 hours. Therefore, the Earth turns 360/24 or 15° in one hour. Every hour, the shadow cast by the gnomon moves 15° around the dial.

BABYLONIAN COUNTING

It's perfect!

Why is a circle made up of 360° instead of a nice round number like 100? It all started with the Babylonians, who lived about 4000 years ago near present-day Baghdad in Iraq. We normally count things in units of 10, but the Babylonians counted in 60s. So they divided the circle into 360 equal parts called degrees (60 times 6). Their method of counting by 60s affects your life in other ways, too — the dials on your clocks and watches are marked into 60 minutes because of Babylonian counting.

The Babylonians found the number 360 handy because so many whole numbers divide evenly into it. Not 7 or 11, but there are 23 other numbers that do. To measure the 360 degrees of a circle, you need a special instrument called a protractor.

4. SPHERES

Spin a coin around fast on its edge. Presto, a sphere or ball-shape — a circle in three dimensions. So what's so special about a sphere? Every place on its outside surface is exactly the same distance away from its center. This means you can cut a slice through a sphere anywhere and always get a circle. Try for yourself by cutting slices through an orange or grapefruit.

The sphere is also special because it's so compact — it has the least possible surface area or outside skin to contain its volume. That's why hibernating bears curl up into balls to sleep through the winter — this way they lose the least body heat and stay warmest. It's also why designers make spherical teapots. Heat is lost from a teapot through its outside surface. A spherical teapot loses its heat slowly because it has the least possible outside surface area.

For most of us, the best thing about a sphere is the way it rolls. With every place on its outside surface the same distance from the center, spheres such as marbles and bowling balls roll smoothly in all directions.

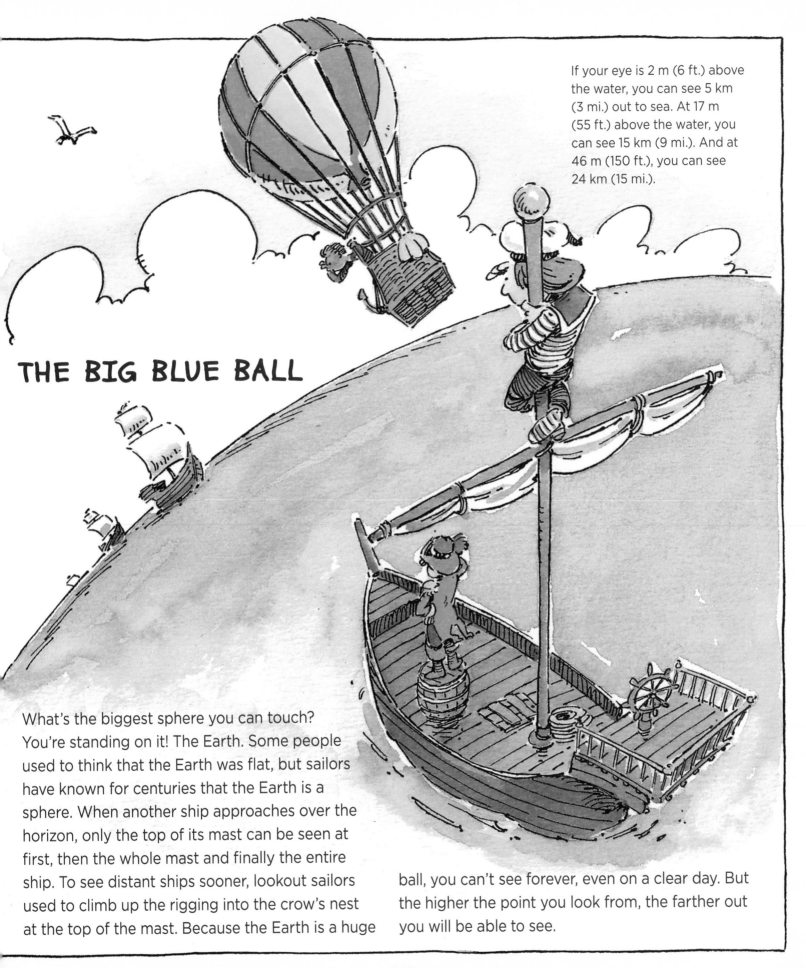

If your eye is 2 m (6 ft.) above the water, you can see 5 km (3 mi.) out to sea. At 17 m (55 ft.) above the water, you can see 15 km (9 mi.). And at 46 m (150 ft.), you can see 24 km (15 mi.).

THE BIG BLUE BALL

What's the biggest sphere you can touch? You're standing on it! The Earth. Some people used to think that the Earth was flat, but sailors have known for centuries that the Earth is a sphere. When another ship approaches over the horizon, only the top of its mast can be seen at first, then the whole mast and finally the entire ship. To see distant ships sooner, lookout sailors used to climb up the rigging into the crow's nest at the top of the mast. Because the Earth is a huge ball, you can't see forever, even on a clear day. But the higher the point you look from, the farther out you will be able to see.

149

Mapping Earth

Take a good look at a world map. It's rectangular with 90° corners, right? So how do you draw a spherical world onto a flat, rectangular map? Find out by turning your breakfast grapefruit into a flat map. Imagine that the grapefruit is the Earth, and the middle of the grapefruit is the equator. The top and bottom of the grapefruit can be the poles.

You'll need:
- a kitchen knife
- a grapefruit
- a cutting board

1. Put the grapefruit on the cutting board and cut it in half.

2. Cut a series of thin slices until you have cut up the whole grapefruit.

3. Cut through the white part between the fruit and the rind, so that you end up with rings of grapefruit rind.

4. Cut through each of the rings to form strips. Lay out all the grapefruit strips as shown.

Your grapefruit map gives you a picture of the surface of the grapefruit. But it doesn't look like a real map because it isn't a rectangle. To make your map rectangular, you'd have to stretch out the shorter strips near the grapefruit's "poles."

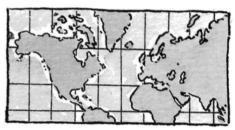

The Dutch mathematician Gerard Mercator was the first mapmaker to solve the problem of showing a spherical world on a flat map. The map he made in 1569 projected the spherical world onto a cylinder. He had to stretch out the top and bottom of his map. That's why places at the Earth's poles, such as Baffin Island and Greenland, look bigger on Mercator maps than they really are in relation to other places.

GREAT CIRCLES

If you cut an orange into slices, which slice would you want? Probably the slice from the middle, because it's the biggest. Circles that go through the center of a sphere are called great circles (all the rest are small circles). A great circle is any circle that divides a sphere into equal halves. The best-known great circle on the planet Earth is the equator. Great circles can be drawn on the globe in any direction so long as they go through the Earth's center. Navigators on airplanes need to know about great circles because flying a great circle route saves fuel. That's because a route on a great circle is always the shortest way between any two points on the Earth's surface.

Bubbles

What's the easiest sphere you can make? The soap bubble. Soap bubbles turn out perfectly round every time. That's because the soap film is like an elastic skin around the air inside. The soap film tries to contract as much as it can, while at the same time the pressure of the air inside is pushing out. So a soap bubble becomes a sphere — the shape with the least possible outside surface area to contain the volume of air inside. Make some perfect spheres every time with this recipe for super bubbles.

You'll need:
- 1 L (4 c.) of lukewarm water
- 150 mL (⅔ c.) of dishwashing detergent
- 15 mL (1 tbsp.) glycerine, available in drugstores (optional, but it makes the bubbles stronger)
- a large, flat container such as a plastic dishpan
- 1 m (3 ft.) of string made of a material that stays wet (cotton and jute work well, but not nylon)
- 2 plastic drinking straws

1. Mix the water, detergent and glycerine gently together in your container. Don't make a lot of suds.

2. Make a bubble frame by threading the string through both straws. Tie the ends together. You now have a giant bubble frame with two straws for handles.

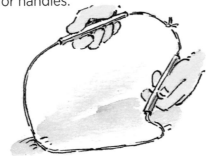

3. Take your bubble mixture and bubble frame outside to blow the bubbles.

4. Wet your hands in the bubble mixture. (Dry hands break bubbles.)

5. Dip the entire bubble frame in the bubble mixture. Lift it out carefully so that you don't break the film.

6. Pull the frame upward over your head or sideways. When your bubble is big enough, close it by bringing your hands together.

P.S. If you want just enough bubble mixture to make small bubbles, you can mix together 250 mL (1 c.) of lukewarm water and 15 mL (1 tbsp.) detergent. For an easy bubble-blower, make two short cuts in the end of a straw and splay out the cut ends.

BUBBLE ARCHITECTURE

Architects call bubbles a "minimal surface" and use bubbles and other soap films to help them design light structures.

Since it's very expensive to send anything into outer space, NASA scientists studied soap bubbles to get ideas for designing light furniture for space stations. Bubbles are useful shapes because they need the least material to enclose the greatest possible volume. The German architect Frei Otto also uses bubbles and other soap films to help him design cheap, strong roofs for large, open areas such as arenas, airports and zoos.

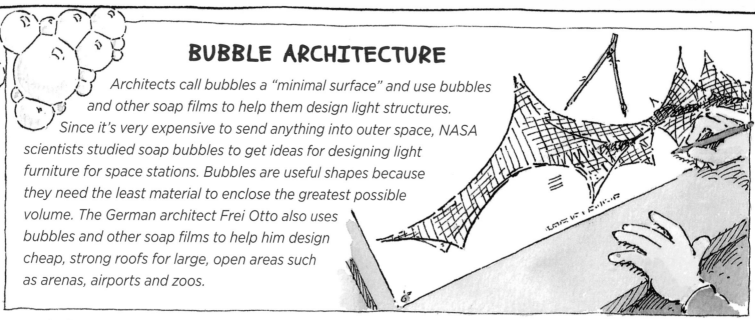

Bubble packing

One bubble is a perfect sphere. But what happens if you have two or three or a whole bunch of bubbles all touching each other? To find out, make some suds.

You'll need:
- some bubble mixture
- a glass
- some water-soluble paint, such as poster paint
- a straw
- some white paper
- waxed paper

I. Put some bubble mixture in the bottom of the glass. Add a small amount of paint and stir.

2. Use a straw to blow into the bubble mixture until bubbles form over the top of the glass.

3. Blow the bubbles off the glass so that they fall on the white paper. Don't let the bubbles fall anywhere else — they'll leave a paint mark. (If the bubble pattern on the paper is too faint, add more paint, stir and try again.)

4. Experiment with different sizes of bubble clusters. When the bubble marks dry, you will be able to see what happens when different-sized bubbles come together.

5. Next put some bubble mixture on the waxed paper to dampen it. (Bubbles won't break on a wet surface.)

6. Put your straw into the bubble mixture. Take it out and blow a single bubble. Place the bubble on the dampened waxed paper.

7. Blow another single bubble and place it carefully beside the first bubble on the waxed paper.

8. Add a third bubble. Notice how the three bubbles come together.

How does it work?

If you had a jar of marbles, you would see air spaces where the marbles do not fit together. Unlike marbles in a jar, bubbles are elastic and can squash together to fill all the empty spaces. Two bubbles come together to share a flat wall. But three bubble walls always meet at 120° angles because this arrangement uses the least amount of bubble film to enclose the air inside.

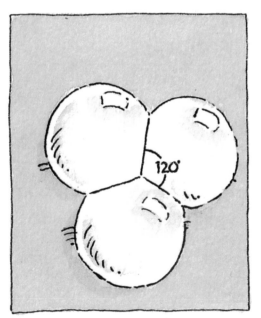

Soap bubbles always come together in threes. You can find this same three-way pattern in honeycomb walls and in mud cracks when mud puddles dry out.

HONEYCOMBS

Take a look at this honeycomb. It sure looks as if bees must be geometry experts to make these honeycomb patterns. Actually, honeycombs form into hexagons exactly the same way that bubble clusters do. The cells of the honeycomb start off as circles. But under the pressure of being packed closely together, the circles flatten out and become hexagonal to fill all the available space.

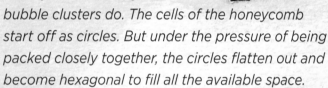

CLOSE PACKING

Scientists study Ping-Pong balls and oranges to discover how shapes fit together to fill space. For example, equal-sized spheres pack together so that each sphere touches or "kisses" 12 others. In this closely packed arrangement, oranges in a crate fill up three-quarters of the space inside — the rest is air.

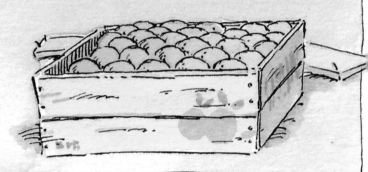

LET'S PLAY BALL!

Which sphere is the most fun? The ball — which comes in all kinds of sizes, colors and materials. Games of marbles, baseball, basketball, tennis, bowling, not to mention golf, Ping-Pong and soccer all use balls. What's so special about the ball? For starters, its center of gravity (balance point) is at its exact center. Check this for yourself by balancing a basketball on the tip of your finger. The trick is to keep your fingertip exactly under the center of the ball.

Rolling games such as marbles, croquet and bowling would be a disaster without the ball. Ever try rolling something rectangular, like a milk carton? Balls roll better than milk cartons because each point on the outside of the ball is the same distance from the center. So balls roll smoothly while milk cartons bump along. Another good thing about the ball is that it touches the ground at only one small point. This cuts down on the drag, or friction, so the ball rolls easily. Give a ball and a milk carton each a good push, and the milk carton soon grinds to a stop while the ball keeps on going.

Losing your marbles

See how far and straight you can shoot in this marble game. People all over the world have played marble games — Aztecs, Romans, Chinese, Africans, Europeans and North Americans. Here's one you can play at home.

You'll need:

- a colored marker
- 6 empty containers of different shapes and sizes, such as milk cartons, cereal boxes and yogurt and ice cream containers
- equal numbers of marbles for each player (5 to 10 marbles per player works well)
- string

3. Agree on a shooting line some distance from the targets such as 3 m (10 ft.) — farther if your players are experts. Mark the starting line with a piece of string.

4. Players take turns shooting one marble at any of the targets. If the marble goes into the container and stays there, the player's score is the number on the container. (It doesn't count if the marble bounces out.)

5. When the players use up all their marbles, they add up their total scores. The one with the highest score wins.

I. Use a colored marker to number each container from 1 to 6 in order of size. Label the biggest container 1, label the next biggest 2 and so on to the smallest container, which is 6.

2. Arrange the containers in a line, alternating bigger containers with smaller ones. These containers will be your targets. Face the open ends toward the shooting line, where the shooters will stand.

SUPER DOMES

What do you get when you cut a sphere in half? Two half spheres (hemispheres) or domes. The dome is one of the strongest shapes there is. Test its strength by squeezing an egg. Put an uncooked egg lengthwise between your palms and push with all your might. You won't be able to break it — honest. The two dome shapes that make up the egg are stronger than you are.

The oldest houses were dome-shaped huts of mud and straw, and we still use dome shapes to make high-tech tents as well as roofs for big sports arenas. Here are some spectacular domes. Can you think of any dome-shaped buildings where you live?

An Inuit family on the move can build an overnight dome, or igloo, of snow blocks in about an hour. First, they outline a circle about 3 m (10 ft.) in diameter. Then they build the igloo from blocks of snow cut carefully to just the right size and shape. The completed dome is strong and can be heated with just one small oil lamp to a comfortable temperature — just below freezing.

Visitors to the World's Fair in Montreal in 1967 were amazed by the American pavilion — a 77-m (252-ft.) steel and Plexiglas bubble, 20 stories high. It seemed to float there as free as a soap bubble, with nothing inside to hold it up. The weight of the building is spread so evenly over the entire base that it doesn't need supporting girders, columns or beams. The American architect Buckminster Fuller invented this spectacular dome, which is very strong but took very little material to build.

S. DISKS

Make a round ball of modeling clay, put it on a table and flatten it out. You've made a disk. This disk has a lot more surface area than your original ball — it takes up more space on the table. Disks are circles with a little thickness to make them three-dimensional. Turned on its rim, a disk will roll like a wheel. Balance a disk such as a paper plate on the tip of your finger and you will discover that its balancing point is the center. Having a disk shape is often an advantage. Round, flat cookies, for example, cook in the oven faster than ball-shaped ones, because they have more surface area exposed to the heat.

Chip disks

These disks are so delicious they don't last long. Experiment with disk-shaped and ball-shaped cookies.

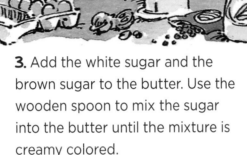

You'll need:

- a large mixing bowl
- a measuring cup
- a wooden spoon
- a mug
- measuring spoons
- a fork
- 2 baking sheets
- a spatula
- oven mitts

- 125 mL (½ c.) softened butter or margarine
- 125 mL (½ c.) white sugar
- 125 mL (½ c.) brown sugar
- 1 egg
- 5 mL (1 tsp.) vanilla
- 2.5 mL (½ tsp.) salt
- 2.5 mL (½ tsp.) baking soda
- 250 mL (1 c.) flour
- 250 mL (1 c.) rolled oats
- 125 mL (½ c.) chopped walnuts or pecans or sunflower seeds (optional)
- 250 mL (1 c.) chocolate chips

1. Ask an adult to turn on the oven to 190°C (375°F).

2. Put the butter (or margarine) in the large mixing bowl.

3. Add the white sugar and the brown sugar to the butter. Use the wooden spoon to mix the sugar into the butter until the mixture is creamy colored.

4. Break the egg into the mug. Add the vanilla, salt and baking soda. Beat together with a fork.

5. Put the egg mixture on top of the butter mixture and beat until well mixed together.

6. Stir in the flour, using the wooden spoon. Add the oats and nuts and stir again.

7. Add the chocolate chips and stir in with the wooden spoon.

8. Roll pieces of the dough into golf-ball-sized balls. Make about 12 balls for each baking sheet.

9. Use the spatula to flatten some balls into disks; leave some as balls.

10. Bake your cookies for 8–10 minutes.

11. Use the oven mitts to take the baking sheets from the oven. Use the spatula to place the cookies on a clean, flat surface to cool.

12. Did the disks or balls cook better? Decide which cookies you like best and bake the rest the same way.

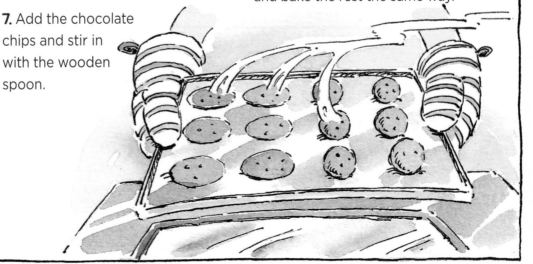

Pinwheel disks

In Holland, rotating disks on windmills use wind power to pump water from low-lying land. Disks catch the wind because, like sails, they have a lot of surface area. In fact, the earliest windmills used canvas sails instead of slatted wooden arms for the rotating disk. Later, wooden arms were mounted on a pivot so that they could always face into the wind. Find out about the power of wind by making this pinwheel disk.

You'll need:
- a piece of thin cardboard
- a pencil
- scissors
- a stapler
- a straight pin
- a plastic straw

I. On the cardboard, draw a square shape as shown and cut it out. A square with a 15 cm (6 in.) side works well.

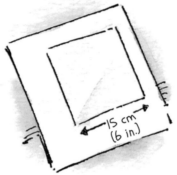

15 cm (6 in.)

2. Cut along the dotted lines as shown.

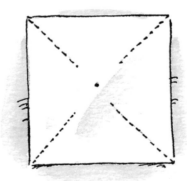

3. Bend the four corners into the center to form a pinwheel and staple it.

4. Push a pin through the center the pinwheel and then through end of a straw.

5. Bend the pin over at the back keep it from falling out.

Blow on your pinwheel. Which direction does it spin — clockwi or counter-clockwise? Which wa does it work better — when you blow from the front or from the side?

SAILING SEEDS

Wind turns windmills and also carries seeds long distances through the air. Since plants are anchored by their roots to one spot, they need to ship off their seeds to open places where new plants can find light and growing space. So some seeds are equipped with special disk-shaped gliding equipment or rotating wings.

• Slippery elm seeds are shaped like disks to glide through the air.

• The maple key's single wing rotates in a circle around the seed so that it spirals downward, slowing its fall. A good breeze can carry maple keys 200 m (665 ft.) away from the parent tree before they reach the ground.

Super flyer

Make your own super flyer to test out how well disks fly.

You'll need:
• scissors
• 2 paper plates
• masking tape

1. Cut the flat center out of one paper plate to produce a plate rim like this.

2. Place the plate and the plate rim together so that the rims touch.

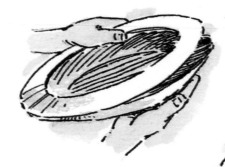

3. Tape the plate to the plate rim using eight short pieces of masking tape as shown.

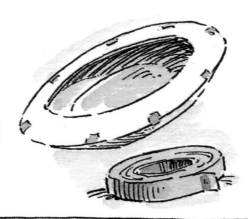

Test this super flyer outside. To launch it, hold it as shown, with your thumb on top and your fingers curled under the rim. Throw it backhand, with a snap of your wrist. With the wind behind it, your super flyer should really zoom.

Experiment with some other disk-shaped flyers that you can find in your own kitchen — plastic plates, metal lids or tops of plastic containers. Give them a test spin to see which ones go farthest. Flying distance will depend on factors such as the size, shape and weight of the disk, your throwing power and, of course, the wind.

Tops

You can turn a disk into a spinning top by putting a stick through its center. Experiment with spinning objects by making this top. If you draw a spiral pattern on your top, it will seem to expand or contract when it spins.

You'll need:

- a compass
- a pencil
- a piece of cardboard
- scissors
- a piece of white paper
- 2 markers of contrasting colors
- glue
- a round cocktail toothpick (not the flattened kind)

1. Use the compass to draw a circle with a radius of 5 cm (2 in.) on the cardboard. Cut out the circle.

2. Draw the same-sized circle on white paper.

3. Color your paper circle. Starting at the circumference, use one of your colored markers to draw a spiral as shown (see page 176 to find out more about spirals). Leave approximately the width of a pencil between each turn, until you reach the center. Go over the colored line with your marker until you have made the colored area just as wide as the white space in between.

4. Fill in the white space with the contrasting color.

5. Cut out the circle and paste onto the cardboard circle to make a colored disk.

6. Use the point of the compass to poke a hole in the center of the disk. Push the toothpick through the cardboard about 1 cm (½ in.). The toothpick works as the axis or pivot for your top.

7. Launch your top. Set it off by spinning it between your thumb and index finger. The more force you apply during the launch, the longer the top will spin. Try clockwise and counter-clockwise spins.

8. Invent your own tops by putting together various handy materials. For a larger top, you can use plastic lids from yogurt containers. Use a pencil instead of a toothpick for the axis.

What makes a difference to how well a top spins? Experiment by raising and lowering the height of the disk on the pencil that is the axis. Make a heavier top by using several layers of material for the disk. Make a top with a bigger diameter.

How does it work?

How long a top will spin depends on its weight, the distribution of the weight and the launch speed. Tops balance better when their weight is kept down low, just as skiers crouch low to keep their balance. Heavier tops spin for longer than light tops, but they are harder to launch. Wide tops spin for longer than narrow tops. And all tops spin faster and longer when launched at higher speeds.

GIANT TOP

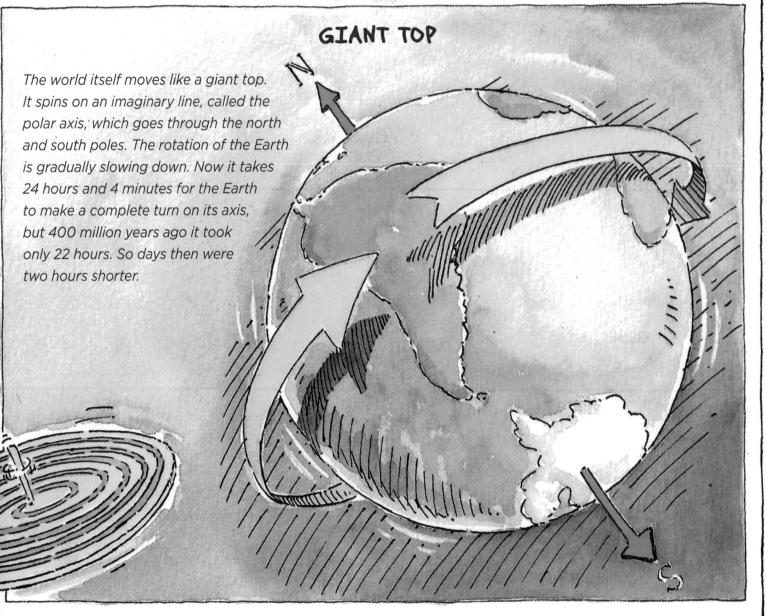

The world itself moves like a giant top. It spins on an imaginary line, called the polar axis, which goes through the north and south poles. The rotation of the Earth is gradually slowing down. Now it takes 24 hours and 4 minutes for the Earth to make a complete turn on its axis, but 400 million years ago it took only 22 hours. So days then were two hours shorter.

WHEELS

What do you think was the most important invention ever? Fire? A metal ax? Ice cream? How about the wheel? Without the wheel, you wouldn't have cups, plates and bowls made on a potter's wheel. There would be no cars, bicycles or skateboards.

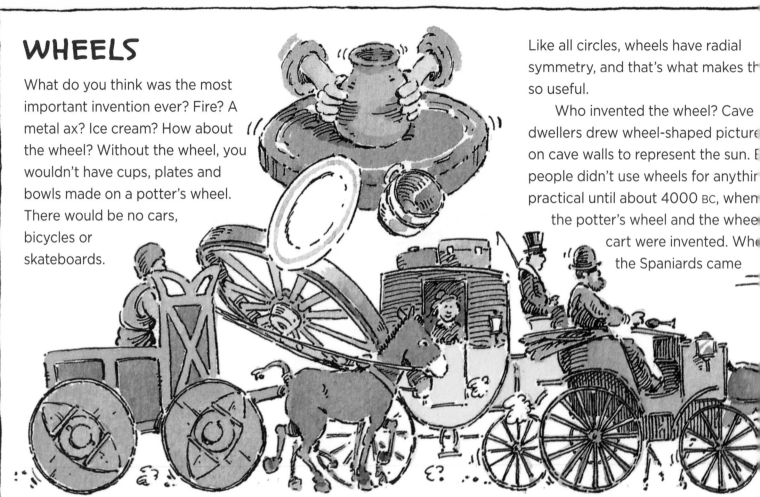

Like all circles, wheels have radial symmetry, and that's what makes th[em] so useful.

Who invented the wheel? Cave dwellers drew wheel-shaped picture[s] on cave walls to represent the sun. [But] people didn't use wheels for anythin[g] practical until about 4000 BC, when the potter's wheel and the whee[led] cart were invented. Whe[n] the Spaniards came

Rollers

Egyptian pyramid builders and the makers of Stonehenge used circular rollers to move huge stone blocks from the quarries to the building sites.

Solid wheels

The first wheels were made of three rectangular boards fastened together into a square and then rounded off at the corners. Early people didn't make wheels from slices of logs because they didn't have metal saws. But cross-sections of logs wouldn't work very well as wheels anyway because they would split apart along the grain.

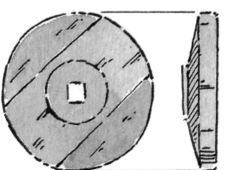

Spoked wheels

Between 2000 BC and 1500 BC, spoked wheels were invented and used for chariots. Made of a hub and rim connected by spokes, these wheels were lighter than solid wheels and provided a faster, smoother ride.

to Mexico after Columbus's discovery of the New World, they were amazed to find that the Aztecs made pottery toys with wheels but they didn't use wheels for transportation. Why not? Because wheeled carts aren't much use unless there are some large, strong, tame animals around to pull them. There were no horses or oxen in North and South America before Europeans brought them across the ocean. So Aztecs used llamas instead and loaded packs on their backs.

The inventor of the wheel figured out that it took less energy to roll something along the ground than to drag it. Wheels work by reducing friction — the result of one thing rubbing over another. Some friction is useful. Without it, your feet would slip out from under you as you walk. (People slip on banana peels because there's not enough friction between the shoe and the banana peel.) But too much friction wastes energy and slows movement. The wheel is the perfect friction beater.

Wheels and axles

The earliest wheels were firmly attached to their axle — when the wheels turned, the axle turned, too. About 100 BC, a big improvement was the rotating wheel that spins freely on an axis that doesn't turn. This design cuts down on friction.

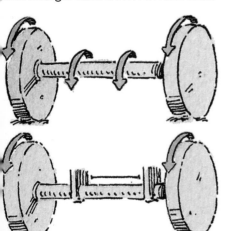

Inflatable rubber tires

John Boyd Dunlop patented the first "pneumatic" rubber tire in 1888 as a way to make bicycles ride more smoothly. Early bicycles were sometimes called "boneshakers" because their metal wheels gave such a bumpy ride, even when covered with solid rubber tires. Dunlop came up with the revolutionary idea of fitting the wheel with an inflatable rubber inner tube protected by a rubber thread.

BACTERIAL WHEELS

No animals have ever evolved wheels to roll on instead of legs. That's because a wheel has to turn freely, like a bicycle wheel, and so it has to be separate from the body. There would be a big problem of connecting the nerves and blood vessels in the wheels to the nerves and blood vessels in the rest of the body. Bacteria have evolved the closest thing to wheel travel. E. coli bacteria move by rotary motion. A threadlike flagellum, like a little tail, rotates at 6000 turns a minute and pushes the bacteria along.

6. CYLINDERS

Can you think of some cylinders in your home? How about cans, paper-towel rolls, broomsticks, pencils, paint rollers and rolling pins? Outside there are tree trunks and telephone poles. And did you know that the long bones in your legs are cylindrical columns? Even polar bear hairs are very thin cylinders, hollow like a drinking straw. Air trapped inside the hair is such a good insulator that it keeps a polar bear's skin warm even in the Arctic.

Cylinders are circles that have been stretched out into a column. The top and bottom of a cylinder are parallel circles. You can make a cylinder by rolling a rectangular piece of paper into a tube, taping the tube together and covering the ends with circles.

A cylindrical soup tin can't hold as much soup as a spherical container would with the same outside surface area. But it's a hit in grocery stores anyway, because its flat bottom keeps it from rolling off the shelf.

Be an architect

If you were an architect and wanted to stay in business, you'd have to design strong buildings that wouldn't fall down. So you'd need to know which shapes support weight best and stand up well to pressure. Try this experiment to find out what shapes make the best supports for buildings.

You'll need:

- 13 × 8-cm (5 × 3-in.) index cards
- masking tape
- a stack of paperback books

1. Form a cylinder by bringing the two short ends of a card together, overlapping slightly. Tape the ends together with masking tape.

2. Now make a square column. Take a second card and make a very narrow fold parallel to one of the short ends. This makes a tab for taping. Now fold the rest of the card in half so that the other short end touches the first fold line. Fold each half in half. Fold your card into a square column and tape down the tab.

3. Now for the triangular column. Take a third card and again make a very narrow fold to form a tab. Fold the rest of the card into three equal sections. Fold into a triangular column and tape down the tab.

4. Test which shape does best under pressure by gently squeezing the sides together.

5. Now test the strength of each of these columns. Carefully, place paperback books, one at a time, on top of one of the columns. Keep adding books until the card collapses; record how many books were supported. (If the column falls over because the books weren't balanced properly, that doesn't count. Try again.) Next test the strength of the other two columns in the same way. Each time, record how many books the column supported. Which shape was the winner?

How does it work?

The strength and stiffness (resistance to bending) of material depend on its shape. The secret to a hollow column's strength is how far its material is spread out from its central axis — the center of the column. In fact, the hollow cylinder is the strongest shape there is. It's a lot stronger than a solid rod made of an equal amount of material. A hollow bamboo stem can grow as high as 37 m (120 ft.) without collapsing under its own weight. The leg bones of the elephant and the brontosaurus are hollow cylinders, too — they'd have to be to support that much weight!

SLICING CYLINDERS

Can you slice a cylinder into these shapes?

You'll need:
- an English cucumber
- a paring knife
- a cutting board

(See page 182)

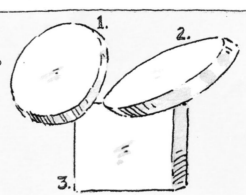

CASTLES

Ever wonder why castles have those grand-looking towers? They actually have a purpose. Builders in Europe started to build more castles with cylindrical towers in the 14th century — just after European armies started using cannons. With this new weapon, an invading army could fire cannon balls at a castle wall from a safe distance, pounding it steadily to pieces. So builders redesigned fortresses with thicker walls and cylindrical towers. Round cannon balls go right through a flat wall. But they tend to roll off a curved cylindrical one.

Cylindrical towers at the corners of a castle have another advantage, too — they're harder to dig under. A favorite trick of attacking armies was to dig a big hole under the castle walls right at the corner. If walls meet to form a corner, then one hole can cause two entire walls to fall down. This doesn't happen so easily when walls are built in a circle.

WHAT'S MY AGE?

You've likely seen a tree stump or the cross-section of a tree, with its many concentric circles. These circles are the tree's growth rings. Each year, a tree grows a new circle outside last year's ring. The ring grows fastest in the spring, slows down in summer and finally stops growing in the fall and winter. Since the rapid spring growth is lighter in color than the slower summer growth, each year's growth shows up as a separate ring. (Except at the equator, of course, where there is no difference in the amount of sunlight during the year and therefore no growth rings.)

If you want to know how old the tree is, you have to count the rings at the base of the tree, not at the top.

That's because a tree trunk grows like an upside-down cone, with a new cone added on top of the old one every year. So there are fewer rings at the top of the tree than at the bottom.

Tricks with cylinders I: Chicken wire

It's easy to roll a flat piece of paper into a cylindrical tube. You can use the tube to spy through or shout through. Or you can use it to make this intricate chicken-wire pattern — it just takes a few pinches.

You'll need:

- a piece of paper (any size from a small square to notepaper size will work)

1. Roll the paper into a tube about 1 cm (½ in.) in diameter.

2. With the thumb and finger of your left hand, pinch one end of the tube to flatten it. Keep pinching with your left hand.

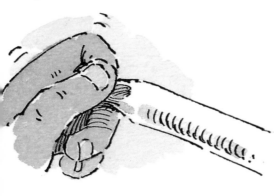

3. With the thumb and finger of your right hand, pinch the tube at right angles to the first pinch. Your second pinch should be as close as possible to the first pinch.

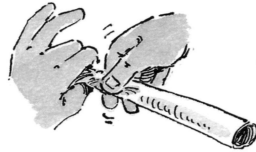

4. Push the two pinches together to make the creases as sharp as you can.

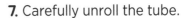

5. Make a third pinch at right angles to the second one. Push the second and third pinches together to sharpen the creases.

6. Continue in this way, making pinches at right angles to the previous one, until you have put pinches in the whole tube.

7. Carefully unroll the tube.

8. If you want to make the pattern easier to see, outline the crease marks with black marker.

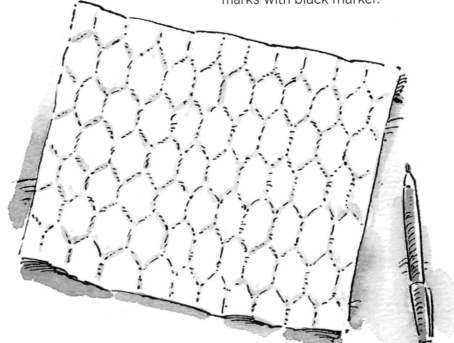

Tricks with cylinders II: Cylinder cipher

You can send a secret message to a friend using a code invented by the ancient Spartans in Greece. For years they were at war with the citizens of Athens. When they wanted to send messages that the Athenians couldn't read, they used a cylinder cipher. They would wrap a leather belt tightly around a stick (called a scytale) and then write on the belt along the length of the stick. When the belt was unwound, all that appeared was a meaningless jumble of letters. But someone with another stick exactly the same size could rewind the belt and read the message. You can make your own version of the Spartan scytale.

You'll need:

paper and scissors
transparent tape
2 new pencils of the same size

Cut a strip of paper about 1 cm (½ in.) wide and 30 cm (12 in.) long.

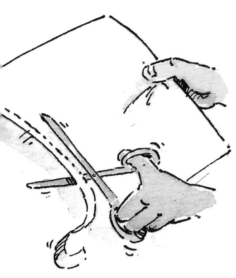

Use tape to attach one end of the strip to a pencil. Wind the strip of paper tightly around the pencil as shown, so that the edges of the paper touch.

3. Secure the other end with tape so that the strip doesn't unwind while you are writing your message.

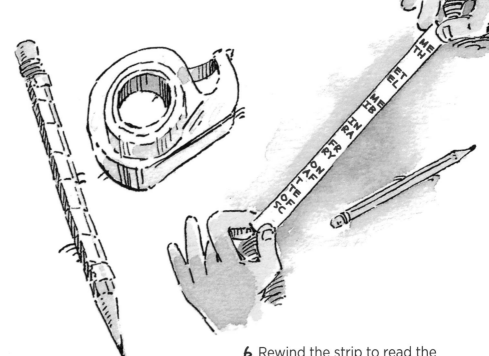

4. Write your message along the length of the pencil. When you get to the end of the line, turn the pencil and start a second line.

5. Unwind the paper strip carefully. Can you read what it says?

6. Rewind the strip to read the message.

You can send messages this way to anyone who knows how to crack the code.

7. CONES

The best thing about cones is that you can put jamocha grape ice cream in them. But there are some more good things about cones:

• The biggest sand pile that you could possibly build on a given area of land would be in the shape of a cone. Volcanoes, which are like giant sand piles, are cone shaped.

• Cones roll, but not in a straight line as spheres and cylinders do. Place a cone on its side, and it will turn in a circle around its pointy end, or vertex. That's why birds that lay eggs on stone ledges often have cone-shaped eggs — these eggs roll in circles around their small end but they don't roll off the ledge.

Cones get top marks for stability. Check this out. Take a cone-shaped drinking cup and try to knock it over.

Cone hats

If you need a special hat for a costume party, start by making a circle, then turn it into a cone.

You'll need:

- a pencil
- string
- large sheets of colored paper (thick paper or Bristol board works well, but you can also use double pieces of newspaper)
- scissors
- sticky tape

1. Use the pencil and string method (page 125) to draw a circle with a radius of at least 25 cm (10 in.). Mark the center of your circle with a dot.

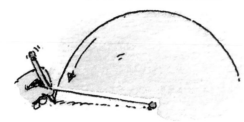

2. Cut out the circle.

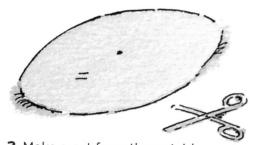

3. Make a cut from the outside of the circle to the center.

4. Give the circle a quarter turn and make a second cut from the outside to the center. Remove the quarter-pie-shaped piece or sector.

5. Tape the edges of the larger piece together. Now you have a sun hat like the hats worn by rice planters in China.

6. If you want a pointier hat, cut out another circle the same size with a radius of 25 cm (10 in.). Cut the circle in half. Tape the edges together and you have a clown's hat. To make a really pointy witch's hat, start with a much bigger circle. The radius of the circle is always the length of the side of the hat. Experiment with different sizes.

7. If you made your hat from newspaper, paint it with poster paint to add some pizazz.

What's happening?

You have turned a two-dimensional circle into a three-dimensional cone. Stand your hat on a table. The point, or vertex, of the cone is directly above the center of the circle that forms the base or bottom of the cone.

SLICING A CONE

If you cut a flat slice off the bottom of a cone, you get a circle. But cones can be sliced in other ways to make some unexpected curves or shapes. An ancient Greek mathematician, Apollonius, discovered these shapes, called conic sections.

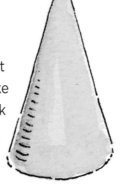

Circle
Make a cut parallel to the base.

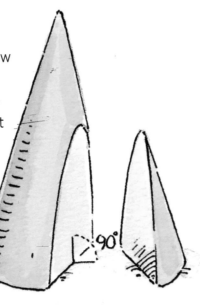

Ellipse
Make a cut at an angle to the base. Kepler discovered that the planets move around the Sun in an ellipse. Halley's Comet makes an elliptical orbit around the Sun, coming back every 76 years close enough for us on Earth to see it.

VOLUME OF A CONE

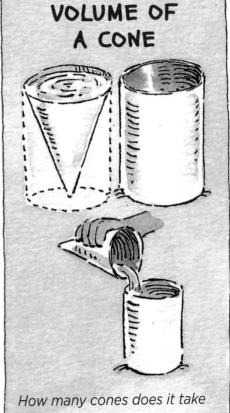

How many cones does it take to fill a cylinder of the same base and height? (See page 182 to find out.)

Hyperbola
Make a cut perpendicular to the base. Some comets follow paths that are hyperbolas. Unlike Halley's Comet, these comets don't come back but keep on going farther and farther into space. The shadow on the wall made by a cylindrical lamp shade is a hyperbola.

Parabola
Make a cut parallel to the side. Water coming out of a hose and balls flying through the air travel in a parabola. Cables supporting a suspension bridge are parabolas.

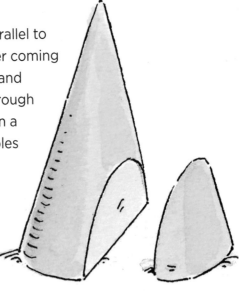

ARCHIMEDES' MIRROR

If you spin a parabola around on its nose, you get a bowl-like shape called a paraboloid. Mirrors in the shape of paraboloids are used in flashlights, headlights and giant telescopes. Why? Because when light hits a parabolic mirror, it bounces off and is focused in one spot. So parabolic mirrors can collect light rays and concentrate their energy to make one strong ray. According to one legend, the famous Greek mathematician Archimedes used parabolic mirrors to fight off Roman ships that had begun a siege of his city of Syracuse in 215 BC. Crafty Archimedes used giant parabolic reflectors to catch the Sun's rays and focus the light on the Roman ships. These intense rays set the ships on fire. Despite the ingenuity of Archimedes, the Romans eventually conquered Syracuse in 212 BC.

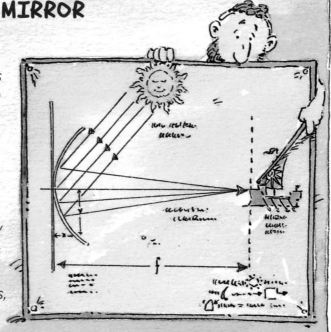

Hyperbola folding

You can make a hyperbola by folding paper.

You'll need:
- a compass
- a pencil
- a piece of paper

1. Use your compass to draw a circle with a radius of about 10 cm (4 in.) on a piece of paper.

2. Choose a point outside the circle and mark it with a dot.

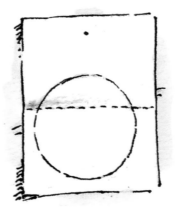

3. Fold the paper so that the circumference of the circle touches the dot. Crease the paper.

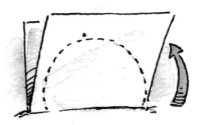

4. Work your way around the circumference of the circle, making more folds in your paper. Make sure that the circumference touches the dot each time.

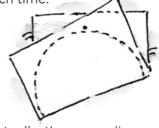

5. Eventually, the crease lines form a hyperbola. As you can see, hyperbolas come in two parts — two curves which are mirror images of each other.

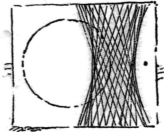

8. SPIRALS

What do a coiled snake and a spider's web have in common? They're both spirals. A spiral is an open curve that keeps on growing. When something grows steadily out from a center, it becomes a spiral — like a spider's web or the horns of a big-horned sheep. Since a spiral doesn't end, it's a good shape for an animal that grows bigger at one end, like a snail. A spiral can also be the shape of a spin — like the water going down a drain or the funnel of a tornado.

Another kind of spiral is the equiangular spiral. Its coils constantly get wider from one turn to the next.

A good example of the equiangular spiral is the snail. As the creature inside grows, it makes its house bigger by adding on new material to the growing edge. The coils get wider as they move out from the center, but the shell itself doesn't change its overall shape. What makes the snail shell coil? The secret to its spiral turning is that the outer edge of its growing surface grows faster than its inner edge. The ram's horn also grows this way into an amazing spiral shape.

But if you think all spirals are the same, look a bit closer. There are really two different kinds of spirals. The Archimedean spiral gets bigger at a steady rate. The distance between each turn stays the same, as it does in a coiled rope. You'll also find the Archimedean spiral in a spider's web. A spider starts her web by spinning out a framework, which she fills in with spokes. Then from the center point, she goes around and around, keeping the same distance between each turn. And then — presto! — an Archimedean spiral just waiting to catch a fly.

Party spiral

Turn this spiral into a party decoration.

You'll need:

- a compass
- a ruler
- a piece of colored paper at least 20 cm (8 in.) square
- scissors
- a piece of thread
- colored markers

1. Draw a circle with a radius of about 10 cm (4 in.) and cut it out.

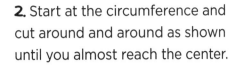

2. Start at the circumference and cut around and around as shown until you almost reach the center.

3. Use the sharp end of the compass to poke a hole through the center.

4. Loop a piece of thread through the hole and hang up your spiral. If you think it needs more pizazz, you can decorate it with markers first. Hang it up over a heat source, and your party spiral will rotate.

FIBONACCI NUMBERS

1 1 2 3 5 8 13 21 34 55 89 144 233 ...
These numbers are special — they follow a pattern. Can you figure out how these numbers are related? (See page 182 to find out if you're right.) This string of numbers, called the Fibonacci number series, gets its name from the greatest European mathematician in the Middle Ages — Leonardo of Pisa, nicknamed Fibonacci, which means son of Bonacci.

But the Fibonacci numbers are not just a neat math trick; they also describe how leaves, flowers and branches grow. Leaves often grow around a central stem in a spiral that follows Fibonacci numbers: five leaves in three turns around the stem, eight leaves in five turns. If you count the petals on flowers, you will discover Fibonacci numbers. The most common number of petals is five. Marigolds and daisies have 13, 21 or 34 petals. (Since daisies usually have 34 petals, which is an even number, you're likely to get bad news when you pull out petals, saying "She loves me, she loves me not.") Try your own petal count of different flowers.

When plants grow by adding on new parts similar to their old parts, they form spirals. Pine cones are spirals and so are the heads of daisies and sunflowers. If you cut through the bottom of a bunch of celery, you find the stalks arranged in a spiral. These spirals are pretty amazing — the numbers of stalks in these spiral arrangements are almost always Fibonacci numbers.

Oh, sunflower!

Check out the Fibonacci series for yourself and grow some birdseed at the same time.

You'll need:

- a place in your garden that gets lots of sun all day
- a trowel or small shovel
- a package of sunflower seeds
- some Popsicle sticks or other markers
- a container of water

I. In the spring when the danger of frost is past, dig some holes about 10 cm (4 in.) deep and 1 m (3 ft.) apart.

2. Put three or four seeds at the bottom of each hole. Cover over the seeds with earth and press the soil down firmly.

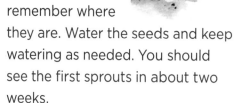

3. Mark the holes where you planted the seeds with a Popsicle stick so that you'll remember where they are. Water the seeds and keep watering as needed. You should see the first sprouts in about two weeks.

4. When the plants are 10 cm (4 in.) tall, remove the smallest, weakest plants to leave just one plant in each hole. This way each plant will have room to grow. Sunflower plants look small at the beginning, but by August they may be 2 to 3 m (6 to 10 ft.) tall!

What's happening?

Watch how the sunflower itself develops. That big disk looks like a single flower, but it's actually hundreds of disk flowers packed together in a head. If you look carefully, you will see that each disk flower is a tube made of five petals fused together. These produce the seeds.

When the disk flowers wither in August, you can see that the seeds are arranged in two interlocking spirals, one whirling counter-clockwise and the other whirling clockwise. Average-size sunflowers have 34 counter-clockwise spirals and 54 clockwise spirals. But some giant sunflowers have 89 spirals and 144 spirals. A Vermont gardener reported a mammoth sunflower with 144 spirals and 233 spirals. Fibonacci numbers again!

A-MAZED

Mazes are tricky paths that you can get lost in. Spiral mazes have an enclosed inner space that is hard to find. You can't go directly to the center, but have to spiral round and round through confusing turns to get there. Once you're inside the maze, it's even harder to find your way back out again. For thousands of years, people have had fun with mazes. They have carved spiral maze patterns onto rock, made mazes from small stones and planted garden mazes.

The most famous maze of all was built by the legendary King Minos of Crete, a large island in the Mediterranean Sea. King Minos hired Daedalus to build a "labyrinth," or maze, to be the home for a monster called the Minotaur. This Minotaur was half man and half bull, very ferocious and very hungry. Young men and women who were put into the labyrinth were his favorite dinner. Finally, Theseus from Athens decided to kill this horrible monster, but he couldn't have done it alone. King Minos's daughter, Ariadne, who loved him, supplied Theseus

with a special sword and a ball of thread. "Tie one end of the thread at the entrance," she said, "and unroll the ball as you go along." When Theseus got to the center of the maze, he killed the Minotaur with Ariadne's sword. Then he escaped from the spiral maze by following the thread back to the entrance.

In memory of the labyrinth of King Minos, people have made labyrinths or mazes that are big enough to walk through. In the Middle Ages, tile mazes were built inside European cathedrals like the one in Chartres Cathedral in France. Later, more affluent people had their gardeners plant hedge mazes on their estates. At Hampton Court Palace near London, England, there is a famous hedge maze with paths almost a kilometer (half a mile) long where thousands of people get lost every year. The next time you go to a sandy beach, you can make a maze for yourself and your friends to get lost in. With a big stick, trace out this spiral design or experiment with designs of your own. Make it tricky to find the correct path into the center and out again.

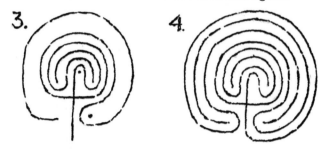

1.

2.

3.

4.

ANSWERS

Squaring off, page 16:

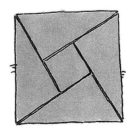

Square takeaway, page 25:

Square numbers, page 18:

When you subtract each square number from the next one in the series, you get: 1, 3, 5, 7, 9, 11, 13, 15, 17, 19 — all odd numbers! So each square number in the series is the sum of successive odd numbers:

1 + 3 = 4
1 + 3 + 5 = 9
1 + 3 + 5 + 7 = 16
1 + 3 + 5 + 7 + 9 = 25

Square mazes, page 34:

In the church maze, the path to the center is long and winding, but you eventually get there because there are few branches and blind alleys. The garden maze is trickier.

Which is bigger?, page 20:

1. Both pieces of cake are the same size. You can see why when you give the inner square a quarter turn. This means that the square outside the circle has twice the area as the square inside the circle.

2. The diagonals of the square and the double ax are exactly the same length.

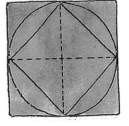

Printing with squares, page 38:

How many squares?, page 22:

There are 30 different squares — 16 squares of 1 square unit; 9 squares of 4 units; 4 squares of 9 units; and don't forget the original square that you started with. (Yep, there are those square numbers again: 16 + 9 + 4 + 1.)

Tangram, page 45:

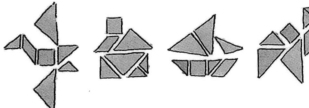

What's my shape?, page 23:

The shape you get is a square.

Square dissection, page 24:

Polyominoes, page 46:

These are the five different tetrominoes.

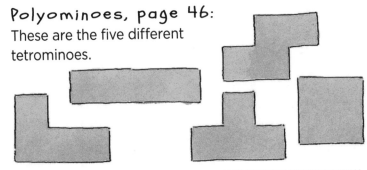

Pentominoes, page 47:

This is just one of the possible answers — there are 2338 other solutions to the rectangle puzzle alone.

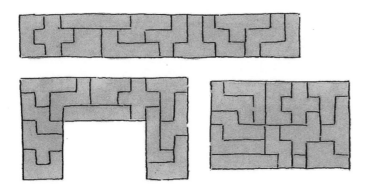

Cube cuts, page 53:

The 1½-cm (1-in.) cube at the center of the bigger cube has six faces, each of which requires a separate cut. So it will take at least six cuts to get the 27 small cubes.

Cross-sections of the cube, page 53:

Slice the cube like this to get these shapes.

Coloring a cube, page 53:

You would need three colors. Since the three faces meeting at a corner need to be different, you can't do it in fewer than three colors. And if you make each of the three pairs of opposite faces the same color, then no adjacent faces are the same.

Rotating a cube, page 53

When you rotate a cube, you get a shape like this:

Prisms and antiprisms, page 57:

The least number of straws needed to make the cube stand up is six.

Find the hidden triangles, page 69:

There are 44 triangles — 16 small triangles, 16 triangles made of 2 small triangles, 8 triangles made of 4 small triangles and 4 big triangles made of 8 small triangles.

Pascal's triangle, page 75:

The next row in Pascal's triangle is:
1 8 28 56 70 56 28 8 1

Turn the triangle around, page 75:

You have to move three coins. Move the coins at the vertices clockwise as shown.

Triangle takeaway, page 77:

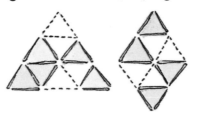

Tetrahedron match-up, pages 112–113:

Match the two square faces together. If necessary, give one of the pieces a 90° turn. As you can see, one of the cross-sections of a tetrahedron is a square.

Grape puzzle, page 113:

Arrange the columns as shown.

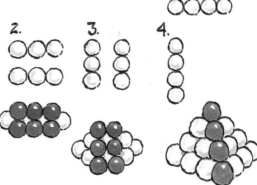

Volume of a square pyramid, page 120:

It would take three square pyramids to fill a square prism. The volume of a square pyramid is one-third the volume of a square prism with the same base and height.

181

Slicing cylinders, page 168:

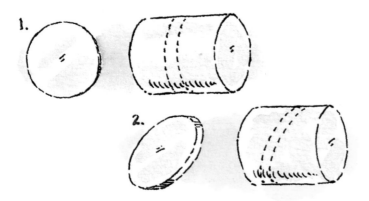

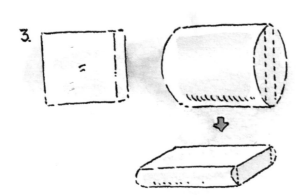

Volume of a cone, page 174:

It would take three cones to fill the cylinder. The volume of a cylinder is exactly three times the volume of a cone with the same base and height.

Fibonacci numbers, page 177:

Each number in the series is the sum of the two previous numbers. Thus, 2 + 3 = 5 and 5 + 3 = 8 and 8 + 5 = 13 and 13 + 8 = 21 and so on.

FORMULAS

Square Formulas

The **perimeter** of a square is 4s (4 × the length of one of its sides).

The **area** of a square is s^2 (the length of one side multiplied by itself).

The **volume** of a cube is s^3 (side × side × side).

Triangle Formulas

The **perimeter** of a triangle is the sum of the length of its sides.

The **area** of a triangle is ½bh (½ × length of base × height).

The **volume** of a square-based pyramid is ⅓Ah (⅓ × area of base × height).

Pythagorean theorem: In a right-angled triangle, the square formed on the hypotenuse is equal to the sum of the squares formed on the other sides.

Circle Formulas

π is 3.14

The **circumference** of a circle is $2\pi r$ (2 × π × radius).

The **area** of a circle is πr^2 (π × radius × radius).

The **surface area** of a sphere is $4\pi r^2$ (4 times the area of a circle with the same radius).

The **volume of a cylinder** is $\pi r^2 h$ (π × radius × radius × height).

The **volume of a cone** is $\frac{1}{3}\pi r^2 h$ (⅓ × π × radius × radius × height).

The **volume of a sphere** is $\frac{4}{3}\pi r^3$ (4/3 × π × radius × radius × radius).

GLOSSARY

Acute angle: an angle that is less than 90°

Altitude: a line from any vertex that is at right angles, or perpendicular, to the opposite side

Angle: the V-shape formed by two straight lines that intersect at a common point

Antiprism: a polyhedron with two identical, parallel faces, whose other faces are all triangles

Arc: a part of the circumference of a circle

Area: the amount of space inside a closed, flat shape such as a circle or rectangle

Base: the base is usually taken as the lowest side of a polygon or the lowest face of a polyhedron

Bisect: to divide into two equal parts

Chord: a straight line joining two points on the circumference of a circle

Circle: a closed curve drawn so that every point on the curve is the same distance from a fixed point called the center

Circumference: the distance around a circle

Concentric circles: circles in the same plane having the same center

Congruent: having the same size and shape

Degree: a unit used to measure angles, indicated by the symbol °

Diagonal: a line segment, inside a polygon, that joins two vertices

Diameter: a chord that goes through the center of a circle

Edge: a line segment formed where two faces of a solid meet

Ellipse: a closed curve looking like a flattened circle, produced when you slice through a cone at an angle to the base

Equilateral triangle: a triangle with three sides that are the same length

Face: any flat side that makes up a solid figure. In a cube, each of the six square sides is a face.

Geometry: the study of the shape and size of things

Hemisphere: half of a sphere

Hexagon: a polygon with six sides

Hypotenuse: the side across from the right angle in a right triangle

Intersect: to share at least one point in common. For example, two straight lines can intersect at a common point.

Isosceles triangle: a triangle having two sides of equal length

Median of a triangle: a line from any vertex of a triangle to the midpoint of the opposite side

Midpoint: the point that divides a line into two equal parts

Obtuse angle: an angle greater than 90° and less than 180°

Parallel lines: two lines on the same plane that are an equal distance apart

Parallelogram: a closed, four-sided figure having opposite sides parallel

Perpendicular lines: two lines that intersect at right angles or 90°

Pi (π): the number you get when you divide the circumference of a circle by its diameter

Plane: a flat surface

Polygon: a closed, flat shape made of straight lines, such as a triangle, square or hexagon

Polyhedron: a closed, solid shape having polygonal faces, such as a cube or a tetrahdron

Prism: a polyhedron with two identical, parallel faces, whose other faces are all parallelograms

Quadrilateral: a four-sided polygon

Radius: the distance from the center to any point on the circumference of a circle. The plural is radii.

Rectangle: a parallelogram with four right angles. A square is a special case of a rectangle.

Regular polygon: a polygon having all sides the same length and all interior angles the same size

Right angle: an angle of 90°, such as this book's corner or the corner of a square

Rhombus: a parallelogram having four sides that are the same length. A square is a special case of a rhombus.

Rotation: a motion that turns an object around a fixed point or center

Scalene triangle: a triangle in which each side is a different length

Sector of a circle: a pie shape outlined by two radii and an arc of a circle

Similar triangles: triangles that are the same shape, but not necessarily the same size

Solid: a three-dimensional figure, such as a tetrahedron, pyramid, cube, cylinder or sphere

Symmetry: repetition of exactly alike parts either on opposite sides of a line or rotated around a central point

Translation: a motion where each point on a figure moves sideways, or slides, the same distance and the same direction

Triangle: a closed, flat shape with three straight sides

Triangulation: the use of a network of triangles to survey and map out a piece of land

Vertex: a point where two sides of a square or triangle meet, or three edges of a cube meet. The plural is vertices.

Volume: the amount of space inside a solid

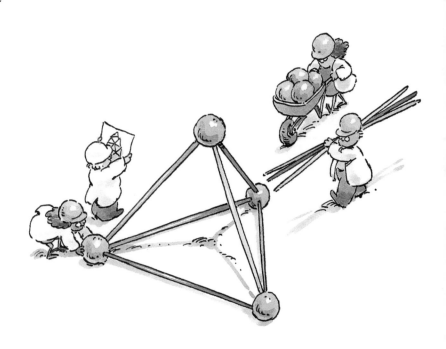

INDEX

A

activities, circles
 blowing bubbles, 151–152
 bubble prints, 152–153
 chocolate chip cookies, 159
 cipher, 170–171
 conical hats, 173
 drawing a circle, 124–125
 drawing an ellipse, 140
 expanding circle trick, 141
 flying disks, 161
 folding a circle, 127
 folding a hyperbola, 175
 hexagon patterns, 169
 marble game, 155
 Moebius strip, 131
 party spiral, 177
 pinwheel, 160
 prints, 134
 slicing cylinders, 167
 strength of shapes, 167
 sundial, 144
 super circle, 137
 symmetry, 133
 tops, 162–163
activities, squares
 construction kit, 54–55
 cubic bubbles, 62–63
 drawing a golden rectangle, 35
 drawing a square, 13
 folding a square, 12
 grid art, 27
 Jacob's ladder, 21
 making a cube (gift box), 50–51
 multiplying the area of a square,
  14–15
 origami, 42–44
 pentominoes, 46–47

printing with squares, 38–39
prisms and antiprisms, 56–58
tangram, 45
tumbling blocks, 37
See also games; puzzles, squares
activities, triangles
 angles of a triangle, 70–71
 area of a triangle, 73
 bisecting an angle, 72
 bridge building, 96
 connect-the-dots game, 74
 construction set, 104–105
 designs using equilateral
  triangles, 86
 folding an equilateral triangle, 87
 growing an alum crystal, 109
 hexaflexagon, 92–93
 kaleidoscope, 103
 Koch snowflake, 91
 paper airplane, 82
 pyramid, 120
 right angle formed by rope
  stretching, 79
 Sierpinski gasket, 91
 testing the strength of a triangle,
  68, 95
 tetrahedral gift box, 111
 toothpick architecture, 115
 triangle tree, 84
 triangles from cardboard strips,
  67
 triangulation, 83
 weaving a triangle, 88–89
 See also puzzles, triangles
airplanes, paper, 82
altitude, 69, 73
Andreae, Johann, 28

angles
 acute, 70
 bisection of, 72
 obtuse, 70
 of a triangle, 71, 76
 of 60°, 85, 86, 87, 92
 of slopee of roofs, 101
 right, 10, 11, 29, 36, 39, 48, 57, 70,
  78–80
 straight, 70, 71
antiprisms, square, 58
Apollonius, 174
Archimedean spiral, 176
Archimedes, 175, 176
architecture, circles
 strength of shapes, 167
 using domes, 156–157
 using soap films, 152
architecture, squares, 9, 32–33,
 60–61
architecture, triangles, 94–101,
 114–115, 121
area of a circle, 126, 128, 136
area of a square, 14–15, 16, 20, 38
area of a triangle, 73
Aztec pyramids, 121

B

Babylonian counting, 147
bacterial wheels, 165
balls, 148, 154–155
base of a triangle, 69
Bell, Alexander Graham, 116–117
Bermuda Triangle, 77
bilateral symmetry, 132–133
bisectors
    of a side, 69
    of an angle, 72
bridges, 96–98
bubbles, 151–153
    cubic, 62–63
buildings, 32–33, 60-61

C

center of gravity
    of a disk, 158
    of a sphere, 150, 154
Chladni figures, 39
chocolate chip cookies, 159
chord, 126
cipher, 170–171
circumference, 126, 128
city planning, 26–31
city squares, 30–31
close packing of spheres, 154
compass, 125–126
cones, 172–175
conic sections, 174
construction kit, 54
Copernicus, 139
crop circles, 143
cross-sections
    of a cone, 174
    of a cube, 53
    of a cylinder, 168

of a sphere, 148, 150
crystals
    cubic, 48
    growing of, 109
cubes, 50–63, 106
    as prisms, 56–58
    coloring of, 53
    cross-sections of, 53
    cutting of, 53
    Delian Cube, 52
    impossible, 59
    in architecture, 60–61
    net for, 48, 50
    packing of, 48, 60
    puzzles using, 53
    rotating of, 53
    Rubik's Cube, 53
    vertices of, 49
cuboctahedra, 54–55
cylinders, 166–171

D

da Vinci, Leonardo, 119
degrees, in a circle, 147
designs
    using equilateral triangles, 85–86
    with circle prints, 134
    See also patterns

diagonals
    of a cube, 53
    of a square, 10, 12, 14, 20, 41
diameter, 126, 128
Dido, 136
die, numbers on a cubic, 51
disks, 158–165
dissection puzzle
    squares, 16, 24, 45
    triangles, 90
division points, 127
dodecahedra, 106
domes, 156–157
dominoes, 46
doubling
    the size of a picture, 27
    story about, 19
    the volume of a cube, 52
drawing
    a circle, 124–125
    a square, 13
    an ellipse, 140
Dunlop, John Boyd, 165

E

Earth as a sphere, 149–150
edges, 46, 49, 58–59
Egyptians, 73, 79, 80, 118, 121
Eiffel Tower, 99
ellipse, 139–141, 174
equiangular spiral, 176
equilateral triangles, 67, 85–93, 104,
    106, 110
Euler's formula, 59
evolution of plants and animals,
    132–133
expressions, using squares, 17

F

faces, 49, 58–59
Fibonacci, 177
Fibonacci number series, 177, 178–179
focus, of an ellipse, 139
folding
    a hyperbola, 175
    circles, 127
    squares, 12
formulas,
    circles, 183
    squares, 183
    triangles, 183
Fowler octagon, 32
fractals, 91
friction, 154, 165
Fuller, Buckminster, 114–115, 157

G

games
    jeu de parquet, 40–41
    pentominoes, 46–47
gift box, cubic, 50–51
Giotto, 124
golden rectangle, 35
Golomb, Solomon, 46
great circles, 150
grids, 20, 27–29
growth rings, 168

H

Halley's Comet, 174
height of a pyramid, 80
hemisphere, 156
Hermann grid, 20
hexaflexagon, 92–93

hexagons, 37, 53, 66, 86, 87, 102, 111, 120, 127, 153–154
honeycombs, 153
hyperbola, 174, 175
hypotenuse, 79

I

icosahedra, 105, 106
impossible triangles, 71, 76
isosceles triangles, 67, 81–84

J

Jacob's ladder, 21
Japanese houses, 33
jeu de parquet, 40–41

K

kaleidoscope, 103
Kepler, Johannes, 139, 174
kite, tetrahedral, 116–117
Koch snowflake, 91

L

labyrinth, 179
Laczkovich, Miklós, 130
Le Corbusier, 32

M

magic squares, 25
mapping, 150
Mathematicians. *See* Apollonius; Archimedes; da Vinci, Leonardo; Euler's formula; Fibonacci; Golomb, Solomon; Kepler, Johannes; Laczkovich, Miklós; Mercator, Gerard; Moebius, August Ferdinand; Newton, Isaac; Pascal, Blaise;

Penrose, Roger; Pythagoras; Rubik, Ernő; Thales; van Ceulen, Leudolph; von Koch, Helge
Maya temple art, 36
mazes, 32, 34, 179
measuring circles, 128
median, 69
Mercator, Gerard, 150
midpoint of a side, 10, 69
minimal surface, 63, 148, 151–153
minimum perimeter, 136
Minos, 179
Moebius strip, 131
Moebius, August Ferdinand, 131
Mondrian, Piet, 36
multiplying the area of a square, 14–15

N

nets
    for a cube, 48
    for a square-based pyramid, 118
    for a tetrahedron, 110
    for a triangular prism, 102
Newton, Isaac, 108
numbers
    square, 18, 180
    triangular, 74–75

O

octagonal buildings, 32
octahedra, 93, 106, 109
octet truss, 114
optical illusions, 20, 37, 76
origami, 42–44
Otto, Frei, 152

P

packing
    of circles, 129
    of cubes, 9, 48
    of spheres, 154
paper folding, 12, 21, 22, 23, 38, 40,
      42–44, 46–47, 69, 73, 81, 82,
      84, 86, 87, 92–93, 95, 104–105,
      111, 112–113, 120, 127, 128, 133,
      141, 167, 169, 175
parabola, 174, 175
paraboloid, 175
parallel sides, 10, 11
parallelograms, 11, 56, 102
Pascal, Blaise, 75
patterns
    using squares, 36–41
    using triangles, 38–39, 40–41
Penrose, Roger, 76
pentominoes, 46–47
perfection, of a circle, 139
perimeter
    of a square, 11
    of a triangle, 69
pi (π), 128–129
pinwheel, 160
planetary paths, 138–139
Platonic solids, 106
polygons, 11, 68, 99, 105, 106
polynominoes, 46–47
printing circles, 134
printing with squares, 38–39
prisms, 56–57, 102–105, 108
protractor, 144–145, 147
Ptolemy, 138–138
puzzles, squares
    coloring a cube, 53
    cross-sections of a cube, 53

    cutting a cube, 53
    dissection, 16, 24, 45
    hidden numbers on a die, 51
    how many squares?, 22
    pentominoes, 46–47
    rotating a cube, 53
    Rubik's Cube, 53
    square into triangle, 24
    square takeaway, 25
    tangram, 45
    what's my shape?, 23
    which is bigger?, 20
puzzles, triangles
    hidden triangles, 69
    stacking spheres into a
      tetrahedron, 113
    tetrahedral match-up, 112–113
    triangle dissection, 90
    triangle takeaway, 77
    turn the triangle around, 75
pyramids, 118–121
    Aztec, 121
    Egyptian, 80, 121
    height of, 80
    square-based, 54–55, 93, 118, 120
Pythagoras, 18, 79
Pythagorean theorem, 79

Q

quadrilaterals, 11
quilt pattern, 37

R

radial symmetry, 124, 132–133, 164
radius, 126, 128, 176
recipe, for chocolate chip cookies,
    159
rectangular prisms, 56
Red Square, 31
Resch, Ronald, 99
Reuleaux triangle, 89
Reutersvärd, Oscar, 59
rhombicuboctahedra, 55
rhombus, 11
right angles, 10, 11, 29, 36, 39, 48, 57
rolling
    of a cone, 172
    of a sphere, 148, 154
    of a wheel, 124, 164–165
rotation, 39, 41, 53
rotation of the Earth, 147, 163
round buildings, 156–157
Rubik, Ernő, 53

S

Safdie, Moshe, 60
scalene triangles, 67
Sierpinski gasket, 91
signs, 135, 164
signs, using triangles, 107
similar triangles, used for measuring
    height, 80
slopes of roofs, 101
space
    covered by circles, 129
    filled by spheres, 154
space-filling, 48–49, 60
    by tetrahedra and octahedra, 114
    by triangular prisms, 102
spheres, 148–157
spinning
    in outer space, 138
    of pinwheels, 160
    of spirals, 176
    of tops, 162–163

spirals, 35, 161, 162, 176–179
square numbers, 18, 180
square prisms, 56
squaring the circle, 130
stability
    of a pyramid, 118
    of cones, 172
    of tops, 163
Stonehenge, 142–143, 164
stories
    about circles, 124, 129, 136
    about squares, 19, 25, 52
    of the labyrinth, 179
strength
    of shapes, 167
    of a tetrahedron, 110
    of a triangle, 68, 94–95, 97, 115
sundial, 144–147
sunflowers, 178–179
surface area
    of a disk, 158

    of a cylinder, 166
    of a sphere, 148, 151
surveying
    into squares, 29
    with triangles, 73, 83
Sydney Opera House, 100
symmetry
    bilateral, 132–133
    mirror, 81, 82
    radial, 124, 132–133, 164
    three-fold, 85–86, 103

T

tangram, 45
tatami, 33
tetrahedra, 93, 106, 110–117
tetrominoes, 46
Thales, 80
three-way intersections, 153
Tiananmen Square, 31
tiling, 87, 99
tops, 162–163
translation (slide), 39
triangles
    as a cross-section of a cube, 53
    as faces of a polyhedron, 54–55,
      58
    as formed from folding a square,
      12
    patterns using, 38–39, 40–41
    rigidity of, 57
triangular numbers, 74–75
triangular prisms, 55–56
triangulation, in surveying, 73, 83
trominoes, 46
truss, 97–98, 100

U

Utzon, Jørn, 100

V

van Ceulen, Leudolph, 129
Vegreville giant egg, 99
vertices, 10, 49, 55, 58–59, 69

volume
    of a cone, 172, 174
    of a cube, 52
    of a cylinder, 166
    of a sphere, 148
    of a square-based pyramid, 120
von Koch, Helge, 91

W

weaving, 88–89
weight, distribution of, 163
wheels, 124, 164–165

X

Xed-frames, 100